British Army Yearbook 2023

Regiments – Operations – Ceremonial – Future Plans

4   Editors Intro

The British Army's Year

6   General Sanders Looks Ahead
10   In the News
14   British Army and Ukraine War
18   Sudan and Turkey:
     Global Operations
20   Burying a Queen...
     Crowning a King

On This Day

24   Invasion Sicily 1943
26   End of Conscription 1963
28   Operation Telic Iraq 2003

Army Structure

30   The British Army Today
32   Brigades and Divisions
34   Allied Power
35   Global Hubs

The Regiments and Corps

38   The British Army's
     Regiments and Corps
40   Royal Armoured Corps
48   The Infantry
74   Special Operations Forces
76   Special Forces
78   Royal Artillery
88   Army Air Corps
92   Royal Engineers
98   Royal Logistic Corps
102 Royal Signals
106 Royal Army Medical Corps
108 Specialist Units

Future British Army

110 Looking Ahead

ABOVE: Balaklava Company of the Royal Regiment of Scotland played a central role in the laying in state of Queen Elizabeth II in Edinburgh in September 2022. (MOD/CROWN COPYRIGHT)

ABOVE: Gunners of Royal Artillery on NATO duty in Estonia during the Baltic state's winter. (MOD/CROWN COPYRIGHT)

ABOVE: The Royal Gurkha Rifles are part of the British Army's Global Response Force, 16 Air Assault Brigade Combat Team and are held at high readiness for operations anywhere in the world. (MOD/CROWN COPYRIGHT)

ISBN: 978 1 80282 781 1
Editor: Tim Ripley
Data and image research: Fergus Ripley
Senior editor, specials: Roger Mortimer
Email: roger.mortimer@keypublishing.com
Cover: Steve Donovan
Design: SJmagic DESIGN SERVICES, India
Advertising Sales Manager: Brodie Baxter
Email: brodie.baxter@keypublishing.com
Tel: 01780 755131
Advertising Production: Debi McGowan
Email: debi.mcgowan@keypublishing.com

SUBSCRIPTION/MAIL ORDER
Key Publishing Ltd, PO Box 300, Stamford, Lincs, PE9 1NA
Tel: 01780 480404
Subscriptions email: subs@keypublishing.com
Mail Order email: orders@keypublishing.com
Website: www.keypublishing.com/shop

PUBLISHING
Group CEO: Adrian Cox
Publisher, Books and Bookazines: Jonathan Jackson

Published by
Key Publishing Ltd, PO Box 100, Stamford, Lincs, PE9 1XQ
Tel: 01780 755131
Website: www.keypublishing.com

PRINTING
Precision Colour Printing Ltd, Haldane, Halesfield 1, Telford, Shropshire. TF7 4QQ

DISTRIBUTION
Seymour Distribution Ltd, 2 Poultry Avenue, London, EC1A 9PU
Enquiries Line: 02074 294000.

Welcome

All The King's Men

ABOVE: British and Estonian soldiers during NATO exercises in the Baltic State. The British Army has kept a battleground in the country since 2017 as part of NATO's forward enhanced presence deployments.
(MOD/CROWN COPYRIGHT)

Welcome to the third edition of the British Army Yearbook - your essential guide to the British Army. This annual publication aims to provide a wide readership with an update on what the British Army has been doing over the past year and its future direction, as well as looking back at its illustrious history.

The British Army has been fighting the nation's wars for more than 300 years and it has a reputation second to none as a warrior force. Warfare does not stand still, future battles and wars will not be won by reputations alone. So, today's British Army is aiming to keep itself at the cutting edge of combat tactics and ahead of tomorrow's technology.

In this year's edition, the Chief of the General Staff, General Sir Patrick Sanders, will explain the thinking underpinning the British Army's new direction and his plans for the coming year. Recent events in Turkey and Sudan have seen British soldiers deploy into harm's way in large numbers. First to help with disaster relief after southern Turkey was hit by a massive earthquake and then to rescue UK passport holders from Sudan's civil war.

The Russian invasion of Ukraine has seen continued movement of thousands of British soldiers to Eastern Europe to help defend NATO allies. And tens of thousands of Ukrainian warriors have been brought to Britain to receive military training, which has helped to build a strong bond between the British and Ukrainian armies.

Over the past year, British armoured battlegroups have been exercising

RIGHT: Guardsmen are put through their paces ahead of King Charles III's coronation in May 2023. State ceremonial events are a key role for the regiments of the Household Division.
(MOD/CROWN COPYRIGHT)

LEFT: The Royal Artillery trained Ukrainian soldiers to operate AS90 self-propelled guns given to the country early in 2023 to help it defeat Russian invasion forces. (MOD/CROWN COPYRIGHT)

BELOW: Editor Tim Ripley on tour in Iraq with the King's Own Scottish Borderers. (TIM RIPLEY)

in Estonia and tanks crews from the Royal Armoured Corps joined a Polish brigade for six months, while for the first time British soldiers have taken tanks to Finland as the Scandinavian nation applied to join NATO. At the same time, British logistics troops have been planning and co-ordinating the delivery of allied military aid to Ukraine.

The outbreak of the largest war in Europe since World War Two has seen the Ukrainian and Russian armies locked in intense combat since February 2022 and this has thrown up many lessons that the British Army is taking on board. At the heart of the British Army are its regiments and corps, all of which have distinguished histories of service. So, this year we profile in detail the fighting units of the British Army and their essential support forces. We look back at their history and explain their role in the modern British Army. More details have also emerged about plans announced in 2021 to reorganise the British Army and we detail these developments, which aim to re-equip frontline regiments with a new generation of weapons as well restructure the army's brigades and divisions.

We look back at several famous British Army battles and campaigns to bring alive the experience and sacrifice of past generations of British soldiers. The 60th anniversary of the end of National Service is also referenced.

We hope you find the British Army Yearbook 2023 an informative read and that it stimulates further interest in the organisation as it moves to keep ahead of the latest trends in warfare.

Tim Ripley
Editor
August 2022

General Sanders Charts His Course

Getting Ready for Action

In June 2022 within days of being appointed professional head of the British Army, General Sir Patrick Sanders made headlines when he declared "this is our 1937 moment" and warned of the threat of war in Europe.

Harking back to calls in the 1930s for rearmament to confront the growing threat from Hitler's Germany, Gen Sanders set out his ambition to mobilise the British Army to face new threats while speaking at the Royal United Services Institute (RUSI) Land Warfare Conference.

Gen Sanders returned to RUSI on June 26, 2023 to outline the progress on his efforts to boost the British Army's fighting power. He told the assembled political decision makers, military chiefs, and leading defence academics as this year's conference that there was still much to do to get the British Army ready for action.

LEFT: General Sanders on the road talking to soldiers around the British Army. (MOD/CROWN COPYRIGHT)

"[At last year's Land Warfare Conference] I outlined my first order of the day to the British Army. That we needed a new approach - that we had to mobilise to deter Russian aggression and prevent the spread of war in Europe. We have some way to go, but we have moved out. We are planning to fight differently. And win.

"We have mobilised our equipment. We have led by example, committing British vehicles and weapons to our Ukrainian allies. We have mobilised our training. Well over 17,000 Ukrainians have been trained on British soil and intelligence intercepts tell us that the Russians know when they are fighting soldiers trained here – testament to our instructors' professionalism and Ukrainian tenacity.

"We have mobilised with industry. The purchasing of Archer 6x6 [155mm self propelled guns], signed and sealed within two months, has demonstrated that we can procure rapidly. We have committed to spend over £100 million on Long Range Precision Fires. We have directed almost £200 million to be spent on new Intelligence Surveillance and Reconnaissance [capabilities].

"We have mobilised our productivity. Nine thousand soldiers are currently protecting British interests overseas, with nearly

BELOW: British soldiers headed to Sudan to join the evacuation effort of UK passport holders escaping from the African country's civil war. (MOD/CROWN COPYRIGHT)

6,000 of them in Europe. Today's British Army is the most productive that it has ever been in my 38 years of service; indeed, we have broadly the same number of soldiers currently deployed as we did a decade ago, despite having reduced in size by 21% over that period.

"Internal debate in Russia revolves around how to fight the war more effectively, not how to end it. The Kremlin continues to direct mobilisation. The Russian Army is learning, albeit at a horrendous price. Living standards have not dropped. Russian arms factories are on a war footing, with workers taking on extra shifts to keep the production lines going.

"And Russia is by no means a nation engaged in total war. In the Great Patriotic War [as they call World War Two] Russia dedicated 61% of GDP to the war effort. This so-called special military operation is drawing only three percent of GDP. [Russia] has the means to go much further.

"For UK deterrence to succeed, we need credible armed forces that are balanced across all of the domains. Those who believe that our geography allows us to minimise investment on land or that we can simply hide behind the armies of other NATO contributors are simply wrong.

"Even in the 21st century, an army's credibility will still be measured by how skilfully it can conduct the full orchestra of war – its mastery of combined arms manoeuvre and its ability to integrate with others; for success will only come from being part of a modernised multi-domain force.

"Many of our platforms are outdated and not fit for purpose. I trained on the 432 armoured personnel carrier in the 1980s when it was already 30 years old. It is still in service today. Now change is coming. Over 35 billion pounds is being spent on new equipment over the next 10 years. Thirty five out of our 38 existing platforms are going out of service and being replaced by new capabilities; they will make us one of the most modern, connected, and lethal armies in the world.

"The British Army is restoring momentum – but we must accept that our procurement record has been poor, and our land industrial base has withered. Furthermore, our Army Reserve is not as capable and credible as we need it to be. We must rectify these faults. And there isn't a moment to lose - we must now take the same spirit of mobilisation and turn it towards transformation; the next steps in the reforms that started with Future Soldier.

"We must have the confidence to structure ourselves to meet our core purpose – to fight and win wars on land - and provide genuine utility and credibility to NATO if called upon, while still being able operate

LEFT: British soldiers have joined with allies from around the world, including New Zealand, to train Ukrainians soldiers at facilities in Britain. (MOD/CROWN COPYRIGHT)

globally in support of the United Kingdom's interests.

"So, over the coming months we will uplift the 1 (UK) Division into a credible Land Component Command Headquarters, one capable of integrating effects across all domains. This will include re-subordinating 16 Air Assault Brigade Combat Team under the 1 (UK) Division and looking at how the Army's Global Response Force can contribute.

"We will optimise the 3 (UK) Division to warfight under an enhanced Allied Rapid Reaction Corps. These formations will be at the very heart of our commitment to European deterrence, maximising the opportunity that the new NATO Force Model presents us.

"By the end of this year, Joint Helicopter Command will have evolved into a Joint Aviation Command. This new organisation will pioneer uncrewed aviation into the 2030s, reflecting the emergence of human-machine teaming technology and the rapid proliferation of uncrewed aerial systems.

"We will unlock the true potential of land special operations in enabling the joint force and supporting our NATO allies. 77 Brigade, together with the Army Special Operations Brigade and our Cyber and Electro Magnetic Activities Group, have the potential to be a world leading special operations capability, capable of creating opportunities or constraints in crisis or conflict.

"And, in the spirit of Haldane, our Reserve force will form our second echelon. It is a Reserve that provides our nation with resilience and mass. And by moving away from insisting upon equivalence between our Regulars and Reserves, it will also be one truly designed for our reservists; recognising that they are constrained only by the time they can give, and not by their ambition or desire to serve.

"We will make the British Army more lethal. We have already let [awarded] contracts to replace the ammunition we sent to Ukraine and have committed to increasing our stockpiles of key and general munitions. The next two years will see the delivery of Boxer, Ajax, more than 60 recapitalised M270 Multiple Launch Rocket Systems (MLRS) launchers and Archer [self propelled guns]. We will reprioritise investment towards Remote and Autonomous Systems and dismounted situational awareness capabilities.

"We will continue to enhance our long-range fires capabilities, which enable us to support the other domains from the land, such as through attacking an adversary's air defence or sinking enemy ships. We will invest in air defence, tripling our short range and doubling our medium range capabilities.

"As we are learning in Ukraine, adaptation comes at a cost. A cost in lives.

And with a land war raging in Europe, I would argue we have little excuse for getting it wrong."

The Chief of the General Staff

General Sir Patrick Sanders has been the professional head of the British Army since June 2022. (MOD/CROWN COPYRIGHT)

General Sir Patrick Sanders was born in Tidworth Garrison military hospital and raised in Norway, Gibraltar, and Iraq. He was commissioned in 1986 and spent his early service as an Infantry Officer in The Royal Green Jackets in Germany, Norway, and the UK. He has commanded on operations in Northern Ireland, Kosovo, Bosnia, Iraq, and Afghanistan, including famously leading his battalion for several months during the siege of Basra Palace in Iraq in 2007.

His higher command appointments were 20 Armoured Brigade, the 3rd (UK) Division and the Field Army. He was promoted to General in May 2019 and commanded UK Strategic Command until May 2022. He became Chief of the General Staff in June 2022.

In The News

First Boxer from Telford

MANUFACTURING BEGAN on the British Army's Boxer Mechanised Infantry Vehicle (MIV) at Rheinmetall BAE Systems Land's (RBSL) facility in Telford on March 27, 2023. The last time a platform began manufacture at Telford's Hadley Castle Works site was in 1986 when the production of the Warrior fleet got underway. That veteran vehicle is still in service today.

The Boxer programme will deliver more than 600 vehicles to the British Army. Production has been subcontracted equally between RBSL and Stockport-based WFEL. Both companies will undertake fabrication of the armoured vehicle structures together with assembly, integration, and test of the completed vehicles at their respective facilities. There is additional capacity for further orders and export.

RBSL has invested £40m in its 29-acre site, transforming it into a world-class manufacturing facility so that the business can deliver next generation military vehicles and essential in-service support.

RIGHT: RBSL has begun assembling Boxer armoured personnel carriers at its Telford site. (TIM RIPLEY)

Desert Rats to lead VJTF

Soldiers of the Royal Anglian Regiment will be on NATO duty next year as part of the Very High Readiness Task Force. (MOD/CROWN COPYRIGHT)

A BRITISH Army light mechanised brigade is to provide the framework lead of NATO's Very High Readiness Task Force (Land) (VJTF(L)) during 2024.

The 2024 VJTF (L)'s UK contingent will comprise two light mechanised battalions equipped with Foxhound patrol vehicles, a light cavalry regiment with Jackal patrol vehicles and an artillery regiment equipped with the 105mm Light Gun to provide fire support.

The 7 Light Mechanised Brigade, which is home based at Kendrew Barracks in Cottesmore, Rutland, will have the 2nd Battalion, The Anglian Regiment and the 4th Battalion, The Royal Regiment of Scotland as its infantry component, along with the Royal Scots Dragoon Guards, 4 Regiment Royal Artillery, 32 Engineer Regiment, 6 Regiment Royal Logistic Corps, 1 Close Support Battalion, The Royal Mechanical and Electrical Engineers and 5 Medical Regiment. These units have a normal combined strength of around 3,000 personnel.

Yorkshire Regiment Royally Honoured

KING CHARLES III has honoured The Yorkshire Regiment with the 'Royal' prefix, bestowed in recognition of its exemplary service to the British Crown.

In April the King announced that with immediate effect the regiment will now be known as The Royal Yorkshire Regiment. There will be no change to the regiment's cap badge.

Describing it as an incredibly proud moment, Colonel of The Regiment, Major General Zac Stenning, said: "Today is an historic day. The Royal Yorkshire Regiment is deeply humbled by His Majesty's bestowal of a 'royal' title."

The Yorkshire Regiment was formed in 2006, by the merger of The Prince of Wales's Own Regiment of Yorkshire, The Green Howards (Alexandra, Princess of Wales's Own Yorkshire Regiment) and The Duke of Wellington's Regiment (West Riding) and can trace its history back more than 300 years to 1685.

BELOW: Yorkshire's infantry regiment now has a royal title in honour of its loyal service to the British Crown. (MOD/CROWN COPYRIGHT)

Plasma Project to Save Soldiers' Lives

AN INNOVATIVE project to rapidly deliver blood and plasma to injured soldiers - to save lives in warzones - was given the go ahead in April 2023.

The Ministry of Defence's Blood Far Forward programme aims to deliver blood and plasma within 30 minutes of injury to soldiers wounded in combat.

Dried plasma – which helps the blood to clot – will decrease the army's reliance on frozen plasma which has to be thawed for more than 20 minutes, taking longer to administer, and the new method of distribution could also be used by NHS Air Ambulances in the future.

Technological resources for the project will be provided by Velico Medical, who have been contracted by NHSBT to work in collaboration with NHS scientists, including the process of gaining regulatory approval. The cost of the project is £4.9m.

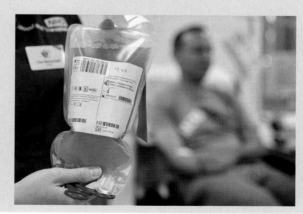

RIGHT: The British Army has introduced a new type of blood plasma to save the lives of soldiers injured in combat. (MOD/CROWN COPYRIGHT)

New Guns for Royal Artillery

THE BRITISH Army will receive new self propelled guns next year to replace those gifted to Ukraine, as part of an agreement struck with Sweden in March 2023.

The first 14 Archer artillery systems will be fully operational with the Royal Artillery by April 2024, forming an interim replacement for the 32 AS90 artillery systems that UK gifted to the Armed Forces of Ukraine in January 2023.

Designed and built by BAE Systems Bofors in Sweden, Archer has double the maximum range of the AS90, greater operational mobility, greater availability, and reduced time into action. Operated by a crew of three or four, it has a lower requirement for personnel than the AS90's five, and benefits from a higher top speed of 70kph compared to the current 53kph.

The purchase of the Archers from Sweden enables the UK to quickly replace AS90 until the long-term Mobile Fires Platform deliveries commence later this decade as part of the Future Soldier modernisation programme.

Tactics and Tech put to Test

AN EXPERIMENTAL company of soldiers from the 2nd Battalion, The Royal Yorkshire Regiment (2 R YORKS) have been exercising on Salisbury Plain Training Area testing new capabilities and innovative equipment as part of the Next Generation Combat Team (NGCT).

Corunna Company Group, 2 R YORKS were embedded into the 1st Battalion The Royal Irish battlegroup during Exercise Wessex Storm in May 2023. They incorporated revolutionary Phalanx Platoons, which is a new concept developed by the Defence Science and Technology Laboratory (Dstl) following research as to 'what a future force might look like'?

Colonel Toby Till from the Experimental and Trials Group described the structure of the NGCT, saying: "It will have an infantry element at the core that is the socket [into which] we are going to plug in a whole range of all arms capabilities."

The soldiers exercised with the latest generation night capability and sighting systems, and the communication systems to enable the Enhance Dismounted Situational Awareness System, which is aimed at improving Command and Control at company level.

Green Energy to Army

A SOLAR farm the size of roughly two football pitches has opened at Duke of Gloucester Barracks in South Cerney. The installation is part of the Army's ongoing effort to improve energy efficiency and support the UK government target of Net Zero by 2050.

Spanning 1.1 hectares and using over 3,000 photovoltaic (PV) panels, the solar farm has been funded under the army's Project Prometheus, a scheme that is increasing renewable energy across the army estate through predominantly ground-mounted solar PV on all suitable sites, delivered by the Defence Infrastructure Organisation (DIO).

Under Project Prometheus, the British Army's first solar farm opened in 2021 at the Defence School of Transport in Leconfield and was delivered by Centrica Business Solutions. The solar farm at Baker Barracks on Thorney Island opened in February 2022 and the final site will open at Rock Barracks in Suffolk this summer.

LEFT: Solar panels are providing power at an increasing number of British Army bases. (MOD/CROWN COPYRIGHT)

Gurkhas Head Down Under

GURKHAS JOINED forces with the Australian Army and US Marines for tough training in the Australian outback near Darwin as part of the British Army's drive to build links with allies in the Indo Pacific region

Deploying from their base in Brunei, C Company 1st Battalion Royal Gurkha Rifles (1 RGR) spent five-weeks participating in Exercise Pacific Kukri.

The open, rocky bush provided an excellent contrast to the claustrophobic jungle the Gurkhas are used to in Brunei, and it tested the full range of their infantry skills. Mounted in Australian Bushmaster protected vehicles, the Gurkhas practised manoeuvring with the support of live mortar and machine gun fire to concentrate force against an objective, and then dispersing to avoid themselves becoming a target.

With temperatures soaring to 38°C, the troops also practised fighting street-by-street and building-by-building through an urban complex, supported by Australian combat engineers to blow entry into buildings and dismantle boobytraps.

ABOVE: The Royal Gurkha Rifles have been training with the Australian Army and US Marines in Darwin as part of Britain's partnerships in the Indo-Pacific region. (MOD/CROWN COPYRIGHT)

British Army and the Ukraine War

Guarding NATO's Eastern Front

RIGHT: Ukrainian artillery crews arrived in Larkhill in January 2023 to begin training on the AS90 155mm self-propelled gun. (MOD/CROWN COPYRIGHT)

With the war in Ukraine more than a year old and showing no sign of coming to any conclusion, the British Army's role in the allied response to the crisis in Eastern Europe has grown dramatically.

As well as providing troops to NATO's enhanced forward battlegroup in Estonia, and participating in allied exercises across Europe, the British Army has played a leading role in training the Ukrainian army and supplying it with modern weapons.

President Volodymyr Zelensky has regularly praised Britain's role in supporting his country's struggle to drive back the Russian invasion since the first British NLAW anti-tank missiles were flown to Ukraine in the days before the war started.

BELOW: British Army instructors from 3rd Battalion, The Rifles, put Ukrainian soldiers through their paces in trench clearing. (MOD/CROWN COPYRIGHT)

Operation Interflex

In the summer of 2022, training areas around Britain started to fill up with thousands of Ukrainian soldiers who had been flown in to begin a crash training programme to prepare them for battle.

Dubbed Operation Interflex, the project involved the Ukrainians being given a crash programme in basic battlefield tactics and survival skills by British Army instructors.

The newly mobilised Ukrainians arrived in Britain on Royal Air Force flights from Poland, carrying little more than the clothes on their backs. British Army quartermasters then equipped them with uniforms, helmets, personal load-carrying equipment, body armour, sleeping bags, and weapons. In a matter of days, they were out on Salisbury Plain, or similar training areas in the north of England, learning how to fight.

Batches of several hundred Ukrainians at a time were cycled through five week long training periods in basic infantry skills, run by training teams directed by 11 Security Force Assistance Brigade. Other Ukrainians were trained to fire 105mm Light Guns, as well as to drive Spartan armoured personnel carriers

and Mastiff mine protected vehicles. At the end of the training period, the British Army and the RAF delivered back to Ukraine a 'combat ready' battalion. By the autumn of 2022, the first British trained Ukrainian battalions were leading the offensives around Kharkov and Kherson. A British trained Ukrainian brigade also played a prominent role in the Battle of Bakhmut in the early months of 2023.

In early 2023, the UK government promised to train 20,000 Ukrainian soldiers during the coming year – double the number of 2022 – and it is ramping up its commitment of personnel to work on Operation Interflex.

During the first six months of Operation Interflex, personnel from several regular infantry battalions were drafted in to assist 11 Security Force Assistance Brigade to run a series of battle camps for the Ukrainians, with 1,000 British soldiers committed to the mission each day for the last half of 2022. The commitment to double the number of Ukrainians under training prompted the British Army to increase the resources involved in Operation Interflex and bring in the army reserve infantry battalions.

LEFT: Ukrainian President Volodymyr Zelensky was hosted at the Armour Centre in Bovington by British Prime Minister Rishi Sunak in February 2023 to see the progress of the training of Ukrainian tank crews. (MOD/CROWN COPYRIGHT)

Reservists from 4th Battalion, The Duke of Lancaster's Regiment (4 LANCS), which is headquartered in Preston and recruits from across the northwest of England, began pre-deployment training in March 2023 to prepare them for their mission over the summer months. Further mobilisations of reserve units and personnel will follow the 4 LANCS commitment as Operation Interflex gathers momentum. Not all the unit's reservists will be on duty for the duration of the mobilisation period, but units will be called in to assist at periods of peak demand.

Arming Ukraine

The British Army has also been steadily emptying its ammunition magazines and vehicles depots to help arm the Ukrainian military. Famously, the British Army sent its first anti tank missiles to Ukraine in the days ahead of the Russian invasion in February 2022 and since then more than 5,361 NLAW anti-armour weapons and 200 Javelin anti-tank missiles have headed east into battle. Starstreak man-portable air-defence systems followed during March and April.

In April 2022, former Prime Minister Boris Johnson promised to supply Ukraine with artillery and other heavy weapons. The Ministry of Defence bought 54 ex-Australian 105mm L119 Light Guns, via BAE Systems, and the Royal Artillery started to refurbish the guns, before they began to train the Ukrainians to operate them.

Six M270B1 Multiple Launch Rocket Systems (MLRS) were delivered during the summer to Ukraine from British stocks after Norway provided three older launchers to replace them in Royal Artillery units. Six Stormer self-propelled HVM air defence systems were also supplied.

A package of surplus armoured vehicles was then delivered to Ukraine during the autumn of 2022, including more than 75 Spartan and over 100 Mastiff vehicles, as well as dozens of Husky-equipped mine protection vehicles.

In January 2023, Prime Minister Rishi Sunak ramped up British support for Ukraine and agreed to supply the country with 14 Challenger 2 tanks and 30 AS90 self-propelled howitzers. Within days, hundreds of Ukrainian soldiers had arrived in Britain to train on the equipment before returning to the front to join the summer 2023 counter-offensive. »

BELOW: The Ukrainian tank crews arrived in the UK on RAF transport aircraft ahead of their crash programme to train them to operate Challenger 2 tanks. (MOD/CROWN COPYRIGHT)

Reinforcing NATO

Not surprisingly, NATO's members in Eastern Europe were increasingly nervous about the threat of the war in Ukraine spilling over into their territory. So, the London government stepped up the British Army's presence in alliance territory to enhance NATO's deterrence mission.

The British battlegroup in Estonia was rapidly reinforced during March 2022 with a battery of MLRS from 19 Regiment RA, as well as an extra infantry battlegroup from the 2nd Battalion, The Rifles, and a battery of 105mm Light Guns from 4 Regiment RA. This later unit was dubbed the Agile Task Force and it spent the summer practicing its role as a rapid reaction force around the Baltic region using RAF Boeing HC6 Chinook heavy lift helicopters.

In February 2022, alliance leaders decided to activate the NATO Reaction Force (NRF) to dispatch reinforcements to alliance members in southeastern Europe. Later in 2022, company-sized detachments from the Royal Irish Regiment and Royal Gurkha Rifles joined the NRF exercises in Bulgaria and Romania, respectively.

Amid the rising tension, neutral Sweden and Finland decided to join NATO and asked the alliance to protect them from Russian attacks or pressure. In an unprecedented move, a squadron of Challenger 2 main battle tanks from the Queen's Royal Hussars (QRH) was dispatched to Finland in May 2022 for Exercise Arrow. Later in the summer, the Agile Task Force also flew to Finland to train with the Nordic country's army.

Poland's geographic position as Ukraine's near neighbour and role as a hub for arms supplies heading to the Ukrainian army meant Britain was keen to help bolster its defence. In February, 16 Regiment RA was dispatched to eastern Poland with its new Sky Sabre air defence missiles to help protect a key airbase where planes carrying arms destined for Ukraine were landed. When Poland transferred scores of its T-72 tanks to Ukraine, the British government ordered another QRH squadron to head to Poland to help fill the gap in Warsaw's army. They stayed in Poland more than six months.

Another first occurred in May 2023, when the 1st Battalion, The Mercian Regiment dispatched a company of armoured infantry and their Warrior infantry fighting vehicles to train in Sweden.

The British battlegroup in Estonia was reinforced in May 2023 to bring it up a full brigade-sized formation, with the arrival of the headquarters of 7 Light Mechanised Brigade Combat Team in the Baltic state for a series of exercise. It was accompanied by the Light Dragoons battlegroup, containing mechanised infantry from the 2nd Battalion, The Royal Anglian Regiment and 4th Battalion, The Royal Regiment of Scotland. The deployment of 7 Brigade was meant to demonstrate that in a time of crisis Britain could rapidly bring its contingent in Estonia to brigade-strength.

The British Army looks set to be on duty in Eastern Europe for many years to come.

ABOVE: Defence Secretary Ben Wallace talks to members of his former regiment, the Scots Guards, during a visit to the British contingent in Estonia in January 2023. (MOD/CROWN COPYRIGHT)

BELOW: British units now regularly train above the Arctic Circle with their comrades from the Norwegian military, including their Leopard tank units. (MOD/CROWN COPYRIGHT)

Sudan and Turkey

British Army Humanitarian Operations 2023

British Army soldiers played a central role in a non-combatant evacuation operation to rescue British passport holders from war-torn Sudan.

Operation Polar Bear got underway on the evening of April 22/23, 2023 to recover a group of diplomats and their families from the British Embassy in Khartoum, with the headquarters of 16 Air Assault Brigade Combat Team deploying to RAF Akrotiri on Cyprus to co-ordinate the complex operation.

US Special Operations Forces Boeing MH-47 Chinook helicopters ferried a team of British soldiers to the US Embassy in Khartoum. After securing the endangered civilians, the British contingent moved in vehicles to Wadi Seidna airbase, north of Khartoum, where RAF Airbus A400M Atlas and Lockheed Martin C-130J Hercules were waiting to extract them to safety on Cyprus.

On April 24, Prime Minister Rishi Sunak ordered the RAF to return to Wadi Seidna to deliver a task force of Royal Marines and British soldiers to set up an evacuation hub to extract thousands of British passport holders and their immediate families. The first troops were flown into Sudan

the following day to kick off the expanded operation. Over the next five days, RAF Hercules and Atlas aircraft shuttled back and forth between Wadi Seidna and RAF Akrotiri, to bring out more 2,000 civilians from the war ravaged country. The precarious state of the runway meant evacuation planners had to look to find an alternative airport in case Wadi Seidna was put out of use. The 700 soldiers of 3rd Battalion, The Parachute Regiment (3 PARA) were forward deployed to Cyprus to be ready to parachute into Sudan to seize an alternative airfield for the RAF evacuation flights.

On the ground in Wadi Seidna, Kingsmen from the Duke of Lancaster's Regiment joined the Royal Marines of 40 Commando in securing the airbase, processing refugees, and helping load them onto RAF aircraft. When the runway appeared to be suffering from damage that threatened to put it out of action, Airborne Sappers from 51 (Parachute) Engineer Squadron flew to Sudan to make critical repairs. The repairs did the trick, and 3 PARA did not need to jump into action.

Concurrently, lead elements of 3 PARA flew into Port Sudan to help set up an additional evacuation hub on the Red Sea coast. This site was used for additional evacuation flights from May 1. By May 2, 2,381 civilians had been evacuated from Sudan on 28 RAF flights.

Turkey and Syria

In February 2023, a huge swath of southern Turkey and Syria was devastated by an earthquake leaving

LEFT: Kingsmen from the Duke of Lancaster's Regiment were part of the security force deployed to Khartoum to oversee the evacuation of British passport holders from the civil war in Sudan.
(MOD/CROWN COPYRIGHT)

an estimated 50,000 people dead and millions homeless. The British Army was in the forefront of Britain's humanitarian response, dispatching medical supplies and personnel to help with the relief effort, as well as deploying the UK's Joint Force Headquarters to co-ordinate British operations in Turkey.

On February 13, RAF Air Mobility Force aircraft began moving the British Army's airborne medics, 16 Medical Regiment –s 16 Air Assault Brigade Combat Team's integral medical unit - bolstered by personnel from the RAF's Tactical Medical Wing, to set up a medical treatment facility in Turkoglu, close to the earthquake's epicentre.

Staffed by more than 70 military clinicians, it provided a surgical capability with two intensive care beds, an emergency department, low dependency ward, two GP-led primary healthcare teams, and a field mental health nurse.

Amid freezing temperatures, the facility was declared ready to receive its first patients on February 14, just over 12 hours after the troops arrived in country. It was located alongside two emergency medical teams - one Turkish and one British - which were funded by the Foreign, Commonwealth and Development Office. The three facilities worked together at the site of a community hospital that was unable to operate due to earthquake damage.

The airborne medics soon began sending a medical outreach patrol out to remote villages in the mountains of Kahramanmaras Province, treating 69 patients over the first two days of the initiative starting. By the time they had returned home to Colchester at the end of March, 13 Medical Regiment had treated more than 6,000 patients.

BELOW: Royal Engineers had to rapidly repair the runway at Wadi Seidna airbase outside the Sudanese capital Khartoum so that RAF evacuation aircraft could continue to evacuate British passport holders.
(MOD/CROWN COPYRIGHT)

Burying a Queen

Queen Elizabeth II's Funeral

ABOVE: The bearer party of The Queen's Company, 1st Battalion, The Grenadier Guards carried Queen Elizabeth II into Westminster Abbey. (MOD/CROWN COPYRIGHT)

RIGHT: The Royal Regiment of Scotland was on parade in Edinburgh's Royal Mile to cheer the proclamation of King Charles III's accession to throne on September 11, 2022. (MOD/CROWN COPYRIGHT)

AFTER QUEEN Elizabeth II passed away at Balmoral Castle in Scotland on September 8, 2022, the machine of the British state swung into action to active Operation London Bridge.

For ten days, the nation showed it's respect to its former monarch and the British Army had a central role in these national events. When the Accession Council met on September 10 in St James's Palace, a contingent of Guardsmen on parade outside raised their bearskins to cheer the new King Charles III.

As The Queen had passed away in Scotland, she was laid in state for a day in St Giles Cathedral in Edinburgh after being carried into the building by a bearer party of the Royal Regiment of Scotland.

The focus of events then moved to London and Queen Elizabeth II's coffin was processed through the centre of the capital to lay-in state in Westminster Hall. She was carried into the building by the Queen's Company of the Grenadier Guards as per the ancient tradition. Members of the Household Division, service chiefs and members of the Royal Family then stood vigil as members of the public viewed their late monarch's coffin.

On the day of the state funeral, the British Army had a key role in the funeral in Westminster Abbey and the subsequent funeral procession to Wellington Arch and then for Queen Elizabeth II's final farewell in St George's Chapel in Windsor.

The procession – which was led by the massed pipes and drums of the Scottish and Irish Regiments, the Brigade of Gurkhas, and the Royal Air Force – included detachments from the armed forces of the Commonwealth, as well as detachments of the British armed forces who held a special relationship with Queen Elizabeth II. Fittingly the Queen's Company of the Grenadier Guards was at the centre of these events and carried their monarch's coffin into St George's Chapel for the final time.

More than 1,000 military personnel joined the funeral procession and some 1,500 soldiers helped with the administration and security of this major national event.

ABOVE: Queen Elizabeth II's coffin was adorned with the Royal Standard flag, a sceptre and orb, and the Imperial State Crown. (MOD/CROWN COPYRIGHT)

LEFT: The final duty for The Queen's Company, 1st Battalion, The Grenadier Guards was to carry their late monarch into the King George VI Chapel. (MOD/CROWN COPYRIGHT)

Crowning a King

King Charles III's Coronation

RIGHT: King Charles III and Queen Camilla made their iconic appearance on the Buckingham Palace after the coronation on May 6, 2023. (MOD/CROWN COPYRIGHT)

BELOW LEFT: Guardsmen based outside London took the train into the capital before parading for King Charles III's coronation. (MOD/CROWN COPYRIGHT)

BELOW RIGHT: Thousands of well wishers braved rain showers in London to cheer on the new King and Queen during coronation day. (MOD/CROWN COPYRIGHT)

ROYAL TRADITION requires that a new king needs to be crowned. The date was set for May 6, 2023, and the ceremonial troops of the Household Division were mobilised to play a starring role in the event.

King Charles III ordered the event and ceremony to be scaled down compared to his mother's coronation in 1953 but it was still the biggest state occasion in several generations.

More than 7,000 military personnel were involved, either in ceremonial roles or to provide security and administrative support. One thousand soldiers and other military personnel lined the route for King Charles III to travel to Westminster Abbey from Buckingham Palace and mounted troops of the Household Cavalry provided an escort.

Once The King had been crowned in Westminster Abbey, he returned to his official residence escorted by a procession of more than 5,000 military personnel, including marching detachments from every regiment or corps of the British Army. They marched behind their regimental colours in a unique ceremonial event. For the first time, the marching contingents all sported

the new regimental insignia bearing the cypher of King Charles III.

Once in Buckingham Palace, the procession moved into the palace grounds and King Charles III then appeared on his residence's rear balcony to receive a royal salute and three cheers from the assembled troops. The cheers were so loud they could be heard down the Mall.

The finale of the coronation was meant to be a flypast by more than 70 aircraft from all three services. However, low cloud prevented the fast jets and large aircraft of the RAF participating so Army Air Corps helicopters had a starring role, leading a formation of RAF and Royal Navy helicopters over Buckingham Palace.

The coronation passed without a hitch – bar the bad weather – and the British Army once again demonstrated its mastery of ceremonial events.

ABOVE: Military personnel on parade for the coronation wore the new royal cipher of King Charles III on their uniforms. (MOD/CROWN COPYRIGHT)

LEFT: After the coronation procession from Westminster Abbey, thousands of military personnel paraded in the garden of Buckingham Palace to cheer the new monarch. (MOD/CROWN COPYRIGHT)

BELOW: Army Air Corps Wildcat and Apache helicopters joined the coronation flypast over Buckingham Palace after bad weather forced RAF fixed wing jets and aircraft to stand down. (MOD/CROWN COPYRIGHT)

Operation Husky

The Invasion of Sicily 1943

ABOVE: Troops from 51st Highland Division unloading stores from tank landing craft on the opening day of the Allied invasion of Sicily, July 10, 1943. (IMPERIAL WAR MUSEUM)

RIGHT: Local children crowd aboard a Sherman tank of the County of London Yeomanry in the village of Belpasso near Catania in Sicily, August 1943. (IMPERIAL WAR MUSEUM)

Eighty years ago, British, Canadian, and American troops made their first successful opposed landing on Axis territory in Europe when they stormed ashore on the Italian island of Sicily.

For over a month, the Allied troops battled German and Italian defenders to gain control of the strategic island and eventually forced the Axis troops to evacuate back to the Italian mainland. This was the first defeat of German troops in a stand-up fight on European territory and it gave the Allies the confidence to press on with landings in Italy a few months later.

For the British Army, it marked the first return to Europe since the 1940 Dunkirk evacuation and allowed many lessons to be learned about how to conduct large scale amphibious and airborne landings.

Operation Husky was the largest amphibious operation of World War Two in terms of size of the landing zone and the number of divisions put ashore on the first day. The plan called for the Allies to land on the southeastern tip of Sicily, with the British 8th Army under Bernard Montgomery landing on the eastern flank to the south of the port of

Augusta and the US 7th Army landing on beaches to the west.

British and American airborne troops kicked off the invasion on the night of July 9/10 to seize key objectives ahead of the amphibious forces. The glider-borne troops of 1st Airlanding Brigade suffered heavily even before they got ashore, with only 12 of the 147 gliders landing on target and 69 crashing into the sea. Over 200 men drowned but the glider troops that did get ashore captured many of their objectives and held out until the 5th Infantry Division got off its beaches and linked up.

Poorly motivated and poorly armed Italian troops put up little resistance to the first landings and soon the allies were racing forward. US troops under the flamboyant tank commander, George Patton headed west and then turned to

clear the north coast of the island. Montgomery's British and Canadian troops advanced north to Catania, to the east of the Mount Etna volcano.

The 1st Parachute Brigade was dropped to capture a key bridge on the line of advance, but the Germans struck back by sending a parachute regiment to counterattack. This was the only battle in World War Two in which both sides air dropped paratroopers into combat against each other. In three days of hard fighting, the British Paras held their German counterparts at bay and were successfully relieved by the tanks of the 8th Army.

By the end of July, the German high command realised that the battle was lost, and they ordered their troops to be evacuated over the Straits of Messina to the Italian mainland. They retreated to Messina and successfully

extracted 52,000 German and 75,000 Italian troops, as well as most of their tanks, vehicles, and other equipment. In the hard-fought battle, the 8th Army suffered 11,843 casualties, including 2,062 killed or missing, 7,137 wounded and 2,644 captured.

The battle was a major boost for the Allies, giving them a vital staging post for the invasion of the Italian mainland in September 1943. For the first time in the war the British Army had taken on and defeated German troops on European territory. Crucially, valuable lessons had been learned about how to organise and execute large scale airborne and amphibious landings that would be put to good use in Normandy less than a year later.

ABOVE: German troops put up fierce resistance after the Allies landed in Sicily and many towns suffered heavy damage during the fighting. (IMPERAL WAR MUSEUM)

LEFT: Italian prisoners of war captured by British troops on Sicily. After Allied troops landed on the Italian mainland in September 1943, the country sued for peace. (IMPERAL WAR MUSEUM)

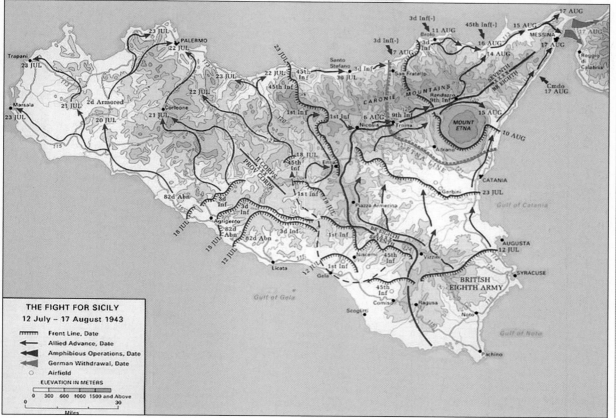

THE FIGHT FOR SICILY
12 July – 17 August 1943

⎓⎓⎓ Front Line, Date
◀— Allied Advance, Date
◀ Amphibious Operations, Date
◀ German Withdrawal, Date
○ Airfield
ELEVATION IN METERS

0 300 600 1000 1500 and Above
0   30
         Miles

LEFT: Operation Husky, July to August 1943. (US ARMY)

Peacetime Conscription

The End of National Service 1963

RIGHT: The Royal Navy relied on press gangs to source recruits during the 17th and 18th centuries, but they were unpopular, and conscription was avoided until World War One. (VAISSEAU DE LIGNE)

BELOW: National Servicemen found themselves on the frontlines of numerous conflicts as Britain withdrew from its empire in the 1940s and 1950s. (MOD/CROWN COPYRIGHT)

Britain has long relied on professional soldiers to fill the ranks of its army. It was a matter of pride for generations that 'free' British subjects volunteered to serve in their military, rather than the nation forcing citizens to wear uniform. The unpopularity of 'press gangs' tricking hapless sailors to serve in the Royal Navy during the Napoleonic wars or recruiting sergeants waving the King's shilling to tempt the unwary to don the red coat had both served to foster the feeling that conscription was just not the British way.

This all changed in 1916 when the horrendous casualties on the western front in France led to the Military

LEFT: National Servicemen on patrol in the Kenyan jungle during the Mau Mau uprising against colonial rule in the 1950s. (IMPERIAL WAR MUSEUM)

Service Act, which introduced conscription for the first time in modern Britain. At the end of the war the act was repealed, and the last conscripts of World War One were demobilised by 1920. Conscription returned in 1939 as World War Two loomed but it was not ended for men when the war ended six years later. Female conscription ended and servicewomen were sent home immediately but rising tension with the Soviet Union meant that Britain could not fully demobilise.

This unprecedented peacetime use of conscription lasted until May 1963, when the last National Serviceman was finally returned to 'Civvy Street'. The 1948 National Service Act had formalised the rules that applied to a whole generation of British young men. From January 1, 1949, healthy males 17 to 21 years old were required to serve in the armed forces for 18 months and remain on the reserve list for four years. Men were exempt from National Service if they worked in one of the three 'essential services': coal mining, farming, and the merchant navy for a period of eight years. If they quit any of those trades early, they were subject to being called up.

In October 1950, in response to the British involvement in the Korean War, the service period was extended to two years and the reserve period was reduced by six months. National Servicemen who showed promise could be commissioned as officers. National Service personnel were used in combat operations, including the Malayan Emergency, the Cyprus Emergency, in Kenya against the Mau Mau uprising, and during the Korean War, where conscripts to the Gloucestershire Regiment took part in the last stand during the Battle of the Imjin River. In addition, National Servicemen served in the Suez Crisis in 1956.

National Service was never popular and so, in 1957, the British government decided to move back to a fully professional armed forces and conscription would be phased out. In November 1960, the last conscripted men entered service, as call-ups formally ended on December 31, 1960, and the last conscripted servicemen left the armed forces in May 1963.

For years after it ended, politicians of all stripes would make calls to 'bring back National Service' as the answer to a variety of social ills. However, while necessity forced the British Army to turn to conscription to fill its ranks in the late 1940s and 1950s, the military top brass was not sorry to see the back of National Service. Two years was not really long enough to train National Servicemen to operate modern equipment and huge numbers of experienced officers and non-commissioned officers were tied up training recruits. It was hoped that a professional army would be able to field better equipment and have better trained soldiers ready for action at short notice. The record of success of the British Army since 1963 would suggest that the ending of National Service was not missed.

BELOW: The end of UK conscription was announced in 1957 and the last National Servicemen returned to Civvy Street in May 1963. (IMPERIAL WAR MUSEUM)

Operation Telic 2003

Britain's controversial war in Iraq saw the British Army take a central role in the ground offensive that opened the way for coalition troops to occupy the country.

ABOVE: When British troops surged into Basra on April 6, 2003, they found the Iraqi military and militia forces had melted away.
(MOD/CROWN COPYRIGHT)

Brigade. A third British land force, 3 Commando Brigade of the Royal Marines, came under the naval command for its initial landing on the al Faw peninsula before it eventually switched to 1 (UK) Division for the final assault on Basra.

The initial incursion into Iraq was made by US Marines and 1 (UK) Division followed on behind, and eventually taking over the American's positions around the western outskirts of Basra city. For just over two weeks, 7 Brigade held a line outside Basra, trading fire with Iraqi troops in the city and staging regular raids into the urban area. Both sides traded artillery and tank fire as they probed for weaknesses. To the north of the city, 16 Brigade sent out ground and air patrols to find and engage Iraqi tank reserves blocking the route into Maysan province. The paratroopers, gunners,

Britain's war in Iraq began in secret during the evening of March 18, 2003, when mobile columns of the Special Air Service (SAS) crossed the Middle Eastern country's western border hunting for Scud missile launchers. Two nights later, the main British land force began crossing into southern Iraq with the objective of capturing the city of Basra to protect the flank of the US Army and US Marines as they headed to Baghdad to depose the country's infamous ruler, Saddam Hussein.

Over the previous two months, just over 20,000 British soldiers of 1 (UK) Armoured Division had arrived in Kuwait to join the US invasion force. Prime Minister Tony Blair ordered the British Army to the Middle East with the objective of disarming Iraq of its arsenal of weapons of mass destruction, which US and British intelligence said he had hidden away in contravention of United Nations mandates. Eventually none were found, which added to the unpopularity of the war.

The British land force comprised the armoured battle groups of 7 Armoured Brigade – the famous Desert Rats – and air and helicopter-borne battalions of 16 Air Assault

RIGHT: Challenger 2 tanks completely outclassed their Iraqi counterparts and none of the British tanks was lost to enemy fire during the brief war fighting phase.
(MOD/CROWN COPYRIGHT)

and helicopter crews of 16 Brigade played 'cat and mouse' with the Iraqi tank crews hiding in the palm groves.

The Battle for Basra reached a climax in the first week of April when resistance to the British raids seemed to weaken. After American troops entered Baghdad, the British commander, Major General Robin Brims, ordered an all-out assault on Basra on April 6. When the first columns of Challenger 2 tanks and Warrior infantry fighting vehicles moved forward, they found the Iraqis troops had melted away. Crowds of cheering civilians met the British columns.

This honeymoon did not last long as the hungry and poverty-stricken citizens of Basra decided to take their revenge on the vestiges of Saddam's regime. Within days anarchy engulfed the city, public buildings were looted, and public utilities started to fail. Soon the city's power and water supplies collapsed, as the summer heat approached.

The British Army had to rapidly switch from war fighting mode into being peacekeepers and humanitarian workers. Engineers and other specialists tried to get Basra back on its feet and British soldiers set up security patrols. It did not take long for the British to be blamed for the chaos and lack of the basics of life across southern Iraq. At the end of June, six Royal Military Policemen were ambushed and killed. Over the next six years insurgents would battle with British troops with increasing intensity, including employing sophisticated roadside bombs to penetrate the armour of British vehicles. By the time the last British troops left Iraq in 2009, 179 British military personnel had died in the country.

LEFT: The 179 British service personnel who lost their lives in Iraq are honoured in this memorial outside the Ministry of Defence in London. (MOD/CROWN COPYRIGHT)

BELOW: A Warrior infantry fighting vehicle of the Royal Regiment of Fusiliers crosses a tank bridge over the Iraqi border as 1 (UK) Division entered the country, en route to Basra. (MOD/CROWN COPYRIGHT)

British Army Today

A Nation's Army

The British Army in 2023 has a central role in defending the United Kingdom and protecting its interests overseas. It is the largest branch of the armed forces with 75,000 trained soldiers in uniform and they are on duty around the world on high profile missions.

At the start of 2023, the British Army boasted 75,710 trained regular, or full time, soldiers. Additionally, there were 24,940 trained members of the Army Reserve who were members of formed reserve units. The number of regular soldiers is set to drop to 73,000 by 2025 under plans announced in the 2021 Integrated Review of British defence and security policy. No soldiers are being made redundant, with the reductions being made by natural wastage through adjustments in recruiting to slow the influx of new soldiers.

Over the past year, the importance of the British Army to national life has been graphically demonstrated by the central role played by thousands

of soldiers in the state funeral for Queen Elizabeth II and then the coronation of King Charles III.

The precision and professionalism of the way the British Army, assisted by its colleagues in the Royal Navy and Royal Air Force, marked transition from one monarch to another was a source of great national pride.

The links between the British Army and its monarch stretch back more than 350 years and several regiments of the modern British Army trace their roots back to the restoration of the British crown in 1660, after the end of Oliver Cromwell's Commonwealth, or republic.

To this day, the monarch remains the commander-in-chief of the British

LEFT: New officers in the British Army now receive the King's Commission. (MOD/CROWN COPYRIGHT)

The day-to-day running of the British Army is exercised by a group, called the Army Board, which sets military regulations, decides on spending priorities and future plans. A government minister chairs the board meetings and then the Chief of the General Staff (CGS), the professional head of the British Army, is responsible for executing them. The CGS heads up the Executive Committee of the Army Board, which is the main command group of the British Army. Sub-groups then overlook specific aspects of activity, such as the Army Dress Committee which has the important role of approving and implementing all aspects of uniforms and how they are worn.

This constitutional position of the British Army means it is a political tool of the government of the day but at the same time long established mechanisms are in place to maintain the established traditions, ethos, and uniforms of the British Army.

armed forces and King Charles III, along with other senior members of the royal family are formal heads of every regiment, or corps, of the British Army. Since the demise of the absolute monarchy, the day-to-day control of the British Army, along with the other armed services, is exercised by government ministers on behalf of 'the Crown in Parliament'.

This constitutional convention means that government ministers set the direction of defence policy, decide on spending priorities, and then issue orders to senior military commanders in time of crisis or war. Parliament votes regularly to renew the legal powers to enforce military discipline, protect official secrets, bylaws protecting military property and to set the number of personnel in each branch of the armed services. The monarch still appoints officers of

the armed forces, by awarding them a King's Commission, but in the case of senior service chiefs, he does so on the advice of the prime minister and the secretary of state for defence.

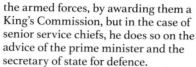

LEFT: Cadets at the Royal Military Academy Sandhurst are put through a demanding training regime to earn the King's Commission. (MOD/CROWN COPYRIGHT)

LEFT: Gurkha soldiers from Nepal have served the British Crown for more than 200 years and are an integral part of the British Army. (MOD/CROWN COPYRIGHT)

Divisions and Brigades

Ready for Action

The British Army currently groups its units into several deployable or operational brigade combat teams and divisions, many of which have long and distinguished histories.

Army Headquarters in Andover is responsible for the peacetime administration of the British Army but for live operations, command of army units switches to tri-service headquarters. The Permanent Joint Headquarters at Northwood near London control overseas missions, and operations within the UK are led by the Joint Standing Headquarters, which is based in the British Army's Headquarters Regional Command in Aldershot.

The British Army's combat, or deployable, divisional headquarters have very different roles. From its base in Bulford on Salisbury Plain, 3 (UK) Division commands units that are trained and equipped to conduct high-intensity armoured combat operations. It is known as the warfighting division and at the end of 2023 there were two main combat or manoeuvre brigades in this division, 12 and 20 Armoured Brigade Combat Teams, supported by 1 Deep Recce Strike Brigade Combat Team.

Intelligence, communications, and information operations units, as well as the newly formed army special operations brigade which controls the Ranger Regiment, are grouped into 6 (UK) Division, which has its headquarters at Upavon.

Units trained and equipped for low intensity combat, peacekeeping, and counter insurgency operations outside Europe, are controlled by 1 (UK) Division from its York-based headquarters. It controls a mix of infantry, engineer, medical, and logistic brigades. These include 4 Light Brigade Combat Team, 7 Light Mechanised Combat Team, 11 Security Force Assistance Brigade and 19 Brigade, which comprises Army Reserve units.

There is a network of army regional commands with subordinate brigade and regional headquarters in Northern Ireland, Wales, Scotland, the Midlands, the Northwest, and the Northeast, the Southeast and the Southwest.

Ceremonial units in the capital are controlled by the historic London District Headquarters, which is

BELOW: British and Danish soldiers from the King's Royal Hussars battlegroup prepare for NATO winter exercises in Estonia. (MOD/CROWN COPYRIGHT)

ABOVE: British soldiers are well respected around NATO for their professionalism, expertise, and experience.
(MOD/CROWN COPYRIGHT)

British Army Division and Brigade Headquarters, July 2023	
Joint Helicopter Command	Andover
1 Combat Aviation Brigade	Middle Wallop
Field Army Troops	Andover
16 Air Assault Brigade Combat Team	Colchester
2 Medical Group	Strensall
Intelligence Surveillance Reconnaissance Group	Larkhill?
Cyber and Electro Magnetic Activities (CEMA) Effects Group	Andover
Land Warfare Centre	Warminster
1 (UK) Division	York
4 Light Brigade Combat Team	Catterick
7 Light Mechanised Brigade Combat Team	Cottesmore
11 Security Force Assistance Brigade	Aldershot
19 Brigade	York
8 Engineer Brigade	Minley
102 Operational Sustainment Brigade	South Cerney
6 (UK) Division	Upavon
Army Special Operations Brigade	Aldershot
77 Brigade	Thatcham
Regional Command	Aldershot
Headquarters London District	London
160 (Welsh) Brigade	Brecon
Headquarters North West & North East	Preston
Headquarters 38 (Irish) Brigade	Lisbon
Headquarters South West	Tidworth
51 Infantry Brigade and Headquarters Scotland	Stirling
Headquarters East & West Midlands	Cottesmore
3 (UK) Division	Bulford
12 Armoured Brigade Combat Team	Bulford
20 Armoured Brigade Combat Team	Bulford
7 Air Defence Group	Thorney Island
25 (Close Support) Engineer Group	Bulford
1 Deep Recce Strike Brigade Combat Team	Tidworth
101 Operational Sustainment Brigade	Aldershot
7 Signals Group	Stafford
1 Royal Military Police Group	Andover
Allied Rapid Reaction Corps	Innsworth
1 Signals Brigade	Innsworth
104 Theatre Sustainment Brigade	South Cerney

located on Horseguards, close to Downing Street, Whitehall, and Buckingham Palace.

The British Army is the lead service for battlefield helicopters across the UK armed forces and the Joint Helicopter Command (JHC) is based inside Army Headquarters. Army Air Corps (AAC), Royal Air Force and Royal Navy officers take turns to command and serve in senior staff jobs in JHC. The 1 Aviation Brigade Combat Team of the AAC reports to JHC, but its units are trained and organised to operate in support of all types of army units.

The British Army's dedicated global response. or theatre entry, unit is 16 Air Assault Brigade Combat Team, and it is kept at high readiness for short notice deployments around the world. It reports direct to Army Headquarters.

BELOW: Armoured units of 3 (UK) Division are held at high readiness for conventional war fighting missions.
(MOD/CROWN COPYRIGHT)

When mobilised for operations and major exercises, divisional and brigade headquarters can take a mix of units and capabilities under command. The warfighting division is configured to control one or more armoured brigade combat teams, as well as,7 Air Defence Group, 25 Close Support Engineer Group and 101 Operational Sustainment Brigade.

The armoured brigade combat teams comprise three or four battlegroups, backed up by supporting reconnaissance, close support artillery, medical evacuation, logistic, surveillance, and aviation support units. The brigade commander is the highest ranking officer who would lead troops into action, with brigade commanders in the 1991 and 2003 Gulf Wars directing operations from the turret of a tank to allow them to view events unfolding in real time.

Allied Power

The British Army's role on NATO's Rapid Reaction Forces

RIGHT: The British Army now has to be ready to deploy around Europe by land, sea, and air in time of crisis. (MOD/CROWN COPYRIGHT)

Britain was one of the founding signatories of the Washington Treaty back in 1949. The meeting established the North Atlantic Treaty Organisation, or NATO, in the early days of Cold War stand-off.

With the collapse of the Berlin Wall in 1989, the British Army of the Rhine was redundant. By 1992, the old 1 (British) Corps had been rebranded as the Allied Rapid Reaction Corps (ARRC). In effect it was NATO's go-anywhere, do-anything headquarters, with a remit to operate both within alliance territory and in humanitarian/peacekeeping missions outside the NATO area.

The British Army was given leadership of the ARRC with a

RIGHT: The Multiple Launch Rocket Systems of the Royal Artillery provide firepower to NATO in Estonia. (MOD/CROWN COPYRIGHT)

BELOW: The ARRC Headquarters is NATO's on-call crisis response force, with communications and intelligence links to co-ordinate a variety of alliance air, land, and sea forces. Major General Mike Keating (right), the ARRC chief of staff, is briefed by his NATO colleagues during the headquarters annual exercise in Cornwall in January 2023. (MOD/CROWN COPYRIGHT)

lieutenant general in command and it also provided the supporting communications, logistics and military police units, under the control of 1 Signals Brigade.

However, the Russian occupation of Crimea in 2014 shocked NATO leaders and the alliance moved to revamp its military forces to enhance the defences of its east European members. The 2014 NATO Summit set up a new NATO rapid reaction unit, dubbed the Very High Readiness Joint Task Force, or VJTF, which was a brigade-sized

force of 5,000 troops, backed by air, naval and special forces. It was to be ready to move within 48 to 72 hours of being alerted. NATO nations take turns to provide the VJTF framework brigade headquarters for a year at a time, as well as the core manoeuvre units.

The British Army is to provide the VJTF headquarters in 2024, in the shape of 7 Light Mechanised Brigade Combat Team. In the spring of 2017, the British Army deployed an 800-strong armoured battlegroup to Estonia under the banner of NATO's enhanced forward presence (EFP) deployment. A light reconnaissance squadron has also deployed to Poland at the same time, working under the US command.

The British Army's presence on the continent changed dramatically in the summer of 2019, when the last units left Germany. Not all British troops returned home, and control was kept of the large vehicle and equipment depot at Ayrshire Barracks in Mönchengladbach and the Dorsten Ammunition Depot.

Access was also secured to the large Sennelager training area. This is intended to allow regular training with NATO allies without having to move large quantities of vehicles and ammunition across the Channel.

Global Hubs

The British Army around the World

They used to say that the sun never set on the British Empire. In the 21st century the British Army no longer guards colonies around the world, but it has an important role in protecting the last handful of overseas territories and several important allies.

As a result, the British Army still has a network of bases in the Far East, Middle East, Africa, Central America, the Caribbean, and the South Atlantic.

In the new jargon introduced in the March 2021 Integrated Review these bases are 'regional hubs' that can be used to project military power, support diplomatic engagement, and help build trade relationships around the world.

The largest permanent overseas British Army presence is in the Mediterranean, where two resident infantry battalions protect the UK sovereign bases on the island of Cyprus.

At the other end of the Mediterranean is the British overseas territory of Gibraltar. It is protected by soldiers of the locally recruited Royal Gibraltar Regiment.

The burden of defending the Falklands Islands in the South Atlantic falls on RAF Typhoons and Royal Navy warships but an infantry company and a battery of Royal Artillery surface-to-air-missiles have a key role securing Mount Pleasant Airport.

The third major foreign garrison is in Brunei where a battalion of Gurkha soldiers protect the sultanate and run jungle-training facilities.

The British Army provides training and administrative support personnel to the defence forces of overseas territories in the Caribbean, including the Royal Bermuda Regiment, the Cayman Regiment, the Turks and Caicos Regiment, and the Royal Montserrat Defence Force.

The biggest British Army overseas training facility is in Canada, where full armoured battlegroups can practice large-scale manoeuvres, but the British Army Training Unit Suffield (BATUS) has been slimmed down in recent years.

Similar facilities exist in Kenya to allow a full infantry battlegroup to conduct live-firing training. Since 2019 the British Army has been expanding its training facilities in Oman, near the port of Duqm, setting up a training area where tanks and other armoured vehicles can exercise in desert conditions.

ABOVE: The Royal Gibraltar Regiment on parade for a royal visitor to 'The Rock' in 2021. (MOD/CROWN COPYRIGHT)

LEFT: Locally recruited volunteers from the Falklands Islands Defence Force assist the British garrison on the South Atlantic islands. In May 2023 they sent a contingent to march in King Charles III's coronation parade. (MOD/CROWN COPYRIGHT)

YOUR GAZINE

Aeroplane traces its lineage back to the weekly The Aeroplane launched in June 1911, and is still continuing to provide the best aviation coverage around. *Aeroplane* magazine is dedicated to offering the most in-depth and entertaining read on all historical aircraft.

shop.keypublishing.com/amsubs

Classic Military Vehicle is the best-selling publication in the UK dedicated to the coverage of all historic military vehicles. From the turn of the 20th century, when warfare started to become increasingly mechanised, right up to the Gulf War of the 1990s, all kinds of military hardware are profiled extensively in every issue.

shop.keypublishing.com/cmvsubs

The British Army's Regiments and Corps

Set to Fight

ABOVE: A classic image of the British soldier as red coated Guardsmen. The British Army honours its ancient traditions and heritage but has to be ready to fight tomorrow's wars. (MOD/CROWN COPYRIGHT)

RIGHT: The Army Air Corps contingent on parade during King Charles III's coronation ceremony. The majority of British soldiers now serve in support and service arms, rather than in long established infantry and cavalry regiments, in line with the changed nature of warfare. (MOD/CROWN COPYRIGHT)

The British Army sets great store by the historical traditions of its famous regiments and their iconic titles. It is, however, a modern fighting force and once in the field it is organised very differently from when in its home barracks.

In peacetime, most soldiers are organised into regiments, or battalions. An infantry regiment comprises one or more battalions, which each have around three or four companies of 150 soldiers. A company is in turn made up of three or four platoons each of some 30 soldiers. Each platoon in turn usually comprises three eight-soldier-strong sections and a small command team. Infantry battalions have several roles. Light role units

march into battle while armoured infantry uses the Warrior infantry fighting vehicle. Light and heavy protected mobility battalions use the Foxhound and Mastiff mine protected vehicle, respectively. Airborne, air assault and light strike units serve in 16 Air Assault Brigade Combat Team. Security Assistance Force battalions train allied forces and public duties units take part in state ceremonial events.

The Royal Armoured Corps and other branches and arms of service, such as the Royal Engineers, Royal Logistic Corps and Army Air Corps (AAC) call their company-sized units squadrons. The Royal Artillery calls its company-sized units batteries. Their platoons are called troops, except in the AAC, where they are called flights. An armoured troop usually has four tanks, and four troops make up a squadron.

Battalion sized units are usually commanded by a lieutenant colonel, company-sized units are led by majors, and platoons are commanded by lieutenants or captains.

Once activated for exercises or operations, infantry battalions or regiments of other combat arms are called battlegroups because they normally have specialist units from other arms attached. So, an infantry battalion could have a squadron of tanks or battery of guns, as well as Royal Engineers, attached for a specific mission to create a battlegroup. The term was adopted because of the way the German army successfully used the concept in World War Two. The US Army uses the term Task Force to describe a combined-arms battalion-sized unit and the British Army is starting to use the designation for units assigned to work under US command.

After the British Army returned all its troops from Germany between 2010 and 2019, it effectively stopped the process of moving units around between garrisons, except for the light role infantry battalions in a rotation schedule to deploy to Cyprus. This old exercise was known as the Arms Plot and saw most regiments and battalions moved between garrisons every two to three years to give troops and their families a chance to live overseas. Now units do not move around, and individuals are moved between units on promotion. This limits disruptions to soldiers' families but means the idea of soldiers serving their entire careers within one unit to build cohesion and *esprit de corps* is now a thing of the past.

The infantry is also uniquely grouped into four administrative divisions - the Guards and Parachute, Union, Queen's and Light – which are not to be confused with operational divisions. These divisions of infantry are used to manage the careers of officers and non-commissioned officers by posting them to new jobs in other units, training establishments or administrative posts. Postings of personnel to the Ranger Regiment are also managed by the infantry divisions of The Infantry.

BELOW: After the accession to the throne of King Charles III, many British Army regiments and corps were updated to include the new monarch's royal cipher. (MOD/CROWN COPYRIGHT)

REGIMENTAL CAP BADGES OF THE BRITISH ARMY

UK MOD Crown Copyright 2023 / Design Studio, Army Media & Comms: ADR010990 AC64697

Royal Armoured Corps

Queen's Royal Hussars
(The Queen's Own and Royal Irish)

THE QUEEN'S Royal Hussars are one of the British Army's three armoured regiments, equipped with the Challenger 2 main battle tank. It is the armoured regiment of 20 Armoured Brigade Combat Team.

The regiment has operated the Challenger 2 for more than two decades and deployed on operations to Iraq with the tank on three occasions between 2004 and 2009. Since 2017, its squadrons have taken turns to be deployed on NATO duty as part of the enhanced forward presence battle group in Estonia.

Queen's Royal Hussars (QRH)	
Successor units at formation	Queen's Own Hussars, Queen's Royal Irish Hussars
Location	Tidworth

During 2022 in response to Russia's invasion of Ukraine the regiment deployed squadron-sized detachments to Finland and Poland. In March 2023, the QRH took over leadership of the NATO battlegroup in Estonia.

The regiment was based in Germany from its formation in 1993 through to 2019 when it re-located to its current home garrison at Tidworth on Salisbury Plain. It is currently configured as a Type 56 regiment, with 56 Challenger 2 tanks. Later in the decade it is to be re-equipped with the upgraded Challenger 3 tank, with a smooth bore cannon and other improved systems.

The QRH is nicknamed 'Churchill's Own', through its affiliation to Winston Churchill, who was commissioned into the 4th Hussars in 1895. The famous World War Two prime minister has been described as 'the greatest Hussar of them all' on account of his swashbuckling military career. Traditions linked to him continue, including the Churchill Cup which is awarded to the top-scoring unit in the regiment's annual gunnery competition and the commanding officer's tank is also named 'Churchill'.

King's Royal Hussars

LEFT: A Challenger 2 of the King's Royal Hussars moving at speed through an Estonian forest. (MOD/CROWN COPYRIGHT)

BELOW: A King's Royal Hussars Challenger 2, flourishing the regimental flag heads the regiment out on a NATO exercise in Estonia. (MOD/CROWN COPYRIGHT)

THE KING'S Royal Hussars currently serve as one of 12 Armoured Brigade Combat Team's two armoured regiments, it is equipped with the Challenger 2 main battle tank.

It was formed in December 1992 in Munster, Germany, and remained there until 2020 when it moved to its current garrison at Tidworth on Salisbury Plain. At first the regiment operated the Challenger 1 tank and deployed to Bosnia with them on NATO peacekeeping duty in 1996.

The regiment conducted three deployments to Iraq between 2003 and 2007 with its Challenger 2 tanks, as part of the British occupation force around Basra.

It has twice led the NATO enhanced forward presence battlegroup in Estonia and its last deployment to the Baltic State started in September 2022. This deployment saw the KRH lead for the first time an armour-heavy battlegroup, with two British and one Danish tank squadrons.

The KRH is currently configured as a Type 56 regiment, with 56 Challenger 2 tanks, but is scheduled to convert later in the decade to the armoured cavalry role, equipped with the new Ajax family of reconnaissance vehicles. Technical problems have delayed the deliveries of the Ajax and there is uncertainty over when the regiment will be converting to its new role.

During the Battle of Vitoria in June 1813, the 14th Light Dragoons captured a silver chamber pot belonging to the Emperor Napoleon from a French baggage train. As a result, the regiment retains the nickname of 'The Emperor's Chambermaids'.

King's Royal Hussars (KRH)	
Successor units at formation	Royal Hussars, 14th/20th Hussars
Location	Tidworth

Royal Tank Regiment

THE ROYAL Tank Regiment has the distinction of being the world's oldest tank unit and traces its history back to 1917 when the Tank Corps was formally formed. This in turn was formed out of the Heavy Section of the Machine Gun Corps, which was set up in 1916 to operate the first ever tanks, or land ships, as they were initially known.

In 1923 it was renamed the Royal Tank Corps and on the eve of World War Two was renamed the Royal Tank Regiment. At its peak

in the war, there were 12 regular and 12 Territorial Army battalions of the RTR. In the modern era, the last two separate RTR units were merged in 2014 to form the single battalion regiment that exists today, with an independent squadron in the Chemical, Biological, Radiological and Nuclear (CBRN) reconnaissance role.

Challenger 2 tanks of 2 RTR spearheaded the invasion of Iraq in 2003 and the regiment's tanks returned to Basra on several

occasions up to 2009 on occupation duty. In 2021, the RTR deployed to Estonia to lead the NATO enhanced forward battlegroup in the Baltic state. Later this decade, the regiment is to receive the upgraded Challenger 3 main battle tank.

Its regimental home continues to be Bovington Camp in Dorset, where the original Tank Corps was formed in 1917, alongside the British Army's Armour Centre, the Armoured Trials and Development Unit and the world famous Tank Museum.

Armoured Cavalry

THE ARMOURED cavalry is the 'eyes and ears' of the British Army's war fighting division. During offensive operations they have the task of seeking out enemy troops and then calling down artillery, rocket, and air strikes against them. When British and Allied troops are on the defensive, armoured cavalry have a key role to play delaying the enemy's advance and inflicting attrition on enemy columns with guided anti-tank weapons.

The 2021 Integrated Review launched a re-organisation of the Royal Armoured Corps to support the new Future Soldier structure, built around two armoured brigade combat teams and 1 Deep Strike Recce Brigade Combat Team. The old formation reconnaissance regiments were now re-titled armoured cavalry regiments. Two of the new regiments were assigned to 1 Deep Strike Recce Brigade Combat Team, with the task of identifying, fixing and then calling down long range fire on enemy forces. It is envisaged that eventually each of 3 (UK) Division's two armoured brigade combat teams will have their own armoured cavalry regiment but at the moment only one regiment operates in this role.

It is still the intention of the British Army that the armoured cavalry regiments will be equipped with the Ajax family of reconnaissance vehicles, but the project has been delayed by technical problems and its fielding schedule for the 589 vehicles is still yet to be confirmed in detail. Until the Ajax is available, the King's Royal Hussars are to continue to operate the Challenger 2 main battle tank.

The three armoured cavalry regiments have been re-organised after the Combat Reconnaissance Vehicle (Tracked) (CVR(T)) family of vehicles was withdrawn from service during 2022. They each have a squadron of Warrior infantry fighting vehicles as a stopgap until the arrival of the Ajax. The other squadrons operate the Jackal wheeled reconnaissance vehicle or are equipped with Javelin and NLAW guided anti-tank weapons.

LEFT: Armoured cavalry regiments now each have one squadron equipped with Warrior vehicles to help prepare crews to operate the new Ajax vehicle, when its technical problems are finally solved. (MOD/CROWN COPYRIGHT)

Household Cavalry Regiment

BELOW: Troopers of the Blues and Royals ride down Whitehall during King Charles III's coronation. Their ceremonial role complements the regiment's operational duties around the world. (MOD/CROWNCOPYRIGHT)

THE SENIOR regiment of the Royal Armoured Corps is the fighting arm of the Household Cavalry. Its personnel are routinely rotating back to ceremonial duties of the Household Cavalry Mounted Regiment in London.

It is intended that the regiment will be the first unit to operate the Ajax vehicle at some point in the near future.

The regiment has seen extensive combat service in Iraq, Afghanistan and elsewhere over the past 20 years. Early in 2023 it deployed to Cyprus as part of the United Nations peacekeeping force on the divided island. It currently serves in 1 Deep Strike Recce Brigade Combat Team.

Household Cavalry Regiment	
Successor units at formation	Life Guards, Blues and Royals
Location	Bulford

Royal Lancers (Queen Elizabeths' Own)

THE ROYAL Lancers famous skull and crossbones cap badge is one of the most recognisable in the British Army and represents its regimental motto, 'Death or Glory'.

Its predecessor unit, the 17th Lancers, were part of the Light Brigade during the Crimean War in the Battle of Balaclava in 1854 and took part in its infamous charge, with the loss of seven officers and 67 men in the debacle.

The regiment has been an armoured cavalry regiment since its formation in 2015. In 2022, it deployed a squadron to Poland as part of NATO's enhanced forward presence battlegroup. It currently serves in 1 Deep Strike Recce Brigade Combat Team.

Royal Lancers (Queen Elizabeths' Own) (RL)	
Successor units at formation	9th/12th Royal Lancers (Prince of Wales's) and the Queen's Royal Lancers
Location	Catterick

RIGHT: The Ajax family of vehicles are to equip the armoured reconnaissance regiments once its technical problems are solved.
(GENERAL DYNAMICS)

Royal Dragoon Guards

THE ROYAL Dragoon Guards was formed in 1992 and initially took on an armoured role equipped with the Challenger 1 main battle tank. It was deployed to Bosnia with its tanks as part of NATO's peacekeeping force.

From 2004 to 2008 it took its Challenger 2 main battle tanks to Iraq as part of the British occupation force. It subsequently deployed to Afghanistan twice between 2010 and 2014 without its tanks, operating in mine protected vehicles.

In 2012, it converted to the CVR(T), and it has since handed in these vehicles for Jackals. During 2021-22 it supplied squadrons to serve as part of NATO's enhanced forward presence battlegroup in Poland. The regiment is now assigned to support 20 Armoured Brigade Combat Team.

Royal Dragoon Guards (RDG)	
Successor units at formation	4th/7th Royal Dragoon Guards and the 5th Royal Inniskilling Dragoon Guards
Location	Warminster

ABOVE: Dismounted action is an integral part of the armoured reconnaissance troopers skill set to allow them to stealthily gather intelligence on the enemy.
(MOD/CROWN COPYRIGHT)

Light Cavalry

AS A result of its combat experience in Iraq and Afghanistan the Royal Armoured Corps formed three regular light cavalry or light reconnaissance regiments. The Army 2020 plan unveiled in 2012 envisaged these regiments would operate in support of 1 (UK) Division, which was tasked with supplying forces required for humanitarian, counter-terrorism, or counter-insurgency missions around the world.

The regiment's main platforms are the Jackal, or Mobility Weapon-Mounted Installation Kit (MWMIK), family wheeled reconnaissance vehicle and its 6 x 6 support variant, known as the Coyote. The upgraded Jackal 2 is now in widespread use in regular units and the original Jackal 1 vehicles are being passed over to Yeomanry units.

The Light Cavalry's operational role is to scout ahead of the main force looking for enemy troops so they can be attacked with ground assaults or artillery fire. Personnel are also trained as forward air controllers so they can rapidly call down air strikes on enemy positions.

LEFT: The Jackal family of reconnaissance vehicles first saw action in Afghanistan and is now the mainstay of regular and reserve light cavalry units. (MOD/CROWN COPYRIGHT)

Light cavalry units are also trained and equipped to escort road convoys through high threat areas and to show presence to reassure local populations threatened by insurgents. Their reconnaissance patrols are provided with enough supplies to be self-sufficient for extended periods away from base.

Between October 2020 and January 2023, the light cavalry regiments supported the British contingent in Mali. Their task was to provide the United Nations peacekeeping force in the North African country with a long-range desert patrol capability.

From March 2017 to August 2021, a Light Cavalry squadron served with the US-led enhanced forward presence battlegroup in Poland.

1st The Queen's Dragoon Guards

THE QUEEN'S Dragoon Guards can trace its history back to 1685 and is the most senior of the British Army cavalry regiments. It is known as the Welsh Cavalry due it its recruitment area in the principality.

Since its formation in 1959, the regiment has been predominately employed in the reconnaissance role apart from brief periods operating Chieftain and Challenger 1 main battalion tanks, in the 1970s and 1990s, respectively.

While attached to 3 Commando Brigade in 2003, the regiment participated in the amphibious landing on Iraq's al Faw peninsula, with is Combat Reconnaissance Vehicle (Tracked) (CVR(T)) being put ashore from landing craft.

In recent years it has served on NATO duty in Poland and supported the United Nations in Mali.

1st The Queen's Dragoon Guards (QDG)	
Successor units at formation	1st King's Dragoon Guards, 2nd Dragoon Guards (Queen's Bays)
Location	Swanton Morley

LEFT: Upgraded Jackal 2 vehicles are now in use with the three regular light cavalry regiments and the Light Dragoons took them to Estonia in May 2023. (MOD/CROWN COPYRIGHT)

Royal Scots Dragoon Guards (Carabiniers and Greys)

THE MODERN day successors, of Scotland's iconic cavalry regiment, The Scots Greys which played a critical role in the Battle of Waterloo in 1815 when it broke up a massive French attack on the British lines. The attack was immortalised in Lady Butler's painting, *Scotland Forever!*, named after the regiment's battle cry as they charged forward.

The current regiment was formed in 1971 and is known in the British Army as the 'Scots DGs', after their official abbreviation.

It was the first regiment to be equipped with the Challenger 2 main battle tank in 1998 and it took the new tanks on their first operational deployment to Kosovo in 2000 and then to Iraq in 2003.

Since 2013 it has been operating in the Light Cavalry role with the Jackal family of vehicles.

Royal Scots Dragoon Guards (SCOTS DG)	
Successor units at formation	2nd Dragoons, 3rd Dragoon Guards, 6th Dragoon Guards
Location	Leuchars

RIGHT: Light cavalry regiments led the British Army's two year-long deployment to Mali to provide the United Nations with a long range reconnaissance capability.
(MOD/CROWN COPYRIGHT)

Light Dragoons

RIGHT: The 1st Queen's Dragoon Guards deployed its reconnaissance squadrons to Mali between June 2021 and May 2022.
(MOD/CROWN COPYRIGHT)

THE MODERN day Light Dragoons maintain the traditions of the Light Dragoons from the 18th century when the British Army formed its first light cavalry regiments.

The current regiment was formed in 1993 and it was immediately deployed to Bosnia as the core of the United Nation Protection Force's Cavalry Battalion or CAVBAT, which operated in the Maglai region. Operational deployments to Iraq and Afghanistan followed between 2003 and 2014.

It is now based in Catterick and is part of 4 Light Brigade Combat Team.

The Light Dragoons were the first light cavalry unit to deploy to Poland in 2017 and Mali in 2020. The regiment deployed in battlegroup strength to Estonia in May 2023 for a major NATO exercise.

Light Dragoons (LD)	
Successor units at formation	13th/18th Royal Hussars (Queen Mary's Own), 15th/19th The King's Royal Hussars
Location	Catterick

Yeomanry

THE RESERVE component of the Royal Armoured Corps is known as Yeomanry and it draws on the centuries old tradition of volunteer cavalry service, with yeomen recruited from Britain's historic counties. The majority of successor Yeomanry units now serve in the RAC, although some of their titles have passed to the Royal Artillery, Royal Signals, Royal Engineer, Royal Logistic Corps and Army Air Corps units.

The modern day Yeomanry is grouped into four main (RAC) regiments, three of which have a light cavalry role. Each of their sub-units, or squadrons, retains the historical title of a predecessor unit. The Queen's Own Yeomanry Scottish and North Irish Yeomanry are assigned to 19 Brigade, as part of 1 (UK) Division. The Royal Yeomanry is assigned to support 1 Deep Strike Recce Brigade Combat Team. Up until 2018, the light

cavalry-role Yeomanry regiments were equipped with the Land Rover Defender-based RWMIK vehicle, and they have since transitioned to the Jackal 1 vehicle as regular units begin to field upgraded Jackal 2 variants.

The Royal Wessex Yeomanry is unique and has the role of augmenting the RAC's Challenger 2 equipped armoured regiments. Its personnel are trained as Challenger 2 crews and, in time of war, would provide each of the armoured regiments with a squadron's worth of soldiers. Many of the regiment's officers and soldiers are former RAC regulars.

Royal Yeomanry (RY)	
Formed	1971
Successor units	Sherwood Rangers Yeomanry, Warwickshire and Worcestershire Yeomanry, Kent and Sharpshooters Yeomanry, Shropshire Yeomanry, Leicestershire and Derbyshire Yeomanry, Westminster Dragoons
Location	Leicester (RHQ)

Queen's Own Yeomanry (QOY)	
Formed	1971
Component units	Yorkshire Yeomanry, The Duke of Lancaster's Own Yeomanry Cheshire Yeomanry (The Earl of Chester's), Northumberland Hussars
Location	Newcastle (RHQ)

Scottish and North Irish Yeomanry (SNIY)	
Formed	2014
Component units	Ayrshire (Earl of Carrick's Own) Yeomanry, North Irish Horse, Fife and Forfar Yeomanry/Scottish Horse, Lothians and Border Horse
Location	Edinburgh (RHQ)

Royal Wessex Yeomanry (RWxY)	
Formed	1971
Component units	Dorset Yeomanry, Royal Wiltshire Yeomanry, Royal Gloucestershire Hussars, Royal Devon Yeomanry, Royal Wiltshire Yeomanry
Location	Bovington Camp (RHQ)

The Infantry

Grenadier Guards

ABOVE: The Queen's Company of the Grenadier Guards carried Queen Elizabeth II to her final resting place in St George's Chapel in Windsor.
(MOD/CROWN COPYRIGHT)

RIGHT: Second Lieutenant Archie Denison-Smith of the Grenadier Guards No 2 Company played a prominent role in King Charles III's coronation.
(MOD/CROWN COPYRIGHT)

THE GRENADIER Guards trace their lineage back to 1656 when Lord Wentworth's Regiment was raised in the Belgian city of Bruges to protect the exiled King Charles II. When he returned to England in 1660 to reclaim the throne, King Charles II was accompanied by his guards, and they protected their new monarch's coronation in Westminster Abbey. The successor unit, which is today the King's Company of the Grenadier Guards, have conducted this role at every coronation since.

The modern King's Company maintains many of its traditions, with the monarch always being known as the 'captain' of the company and members have to be at least six feet tall. When the monarch is female, it is known as the Queen's Company and since the accession to the throne of King Charles III, it has reverted to its title, King's Company. Soldiers of the Queen's Company provided the bearer party at Queen Elizabeth II's funeral in September 2022.

In 1665 the 1st Regiment of Foot Guards was created to bring together the royal guards and this was subsequently titled the Grenadiers in 1815. The modern Grenadiers serve as a light role infantry battalion in 4 Light Brigade Combat Team. It comprises the King's Company, No. 2 Company and The Inkerman Company, a support company with heavy weapons and a headquarters company.

During 2022 the battalion deployed a company-sized group to Iraq to support British forces participating in Operation Shader to counter the remnants of so-called Islamic State (IS).

After 2025, the Grenadiers are to be transferred to London District in the public duties role, participating in state ceremonial events.

The Grenadier Guards (GREN GDS)		
Formed	1665	
Successor units at formation	Lord Wentworth's Regiment, John Russell's Regiment of Guards	
Recruiting areas	National	
Regular Battalion		
Unit	Role	Location
1st Battalion	Light	Aldershot

Coldstream Guards

THE COLDSTREAM Guards is the oldest continuously serving regular regiment in the British Army and it has never been amalgamated.

It was formed as Monck's Regiment of Foot as part of the Roundhead New Model Army and was then renamed The Lord General's Regiment of Foot Guards after it rallied to King Charles II on the restoration of the monarchy in 1660. With Monck's death in 1670, it was again renamed The Coldstream Regiment of Foot Guards after the place in Scotland where it marched from to help restore the crown ten years earlier. Its name was again changed to the Coldstream Guards in 1855 and this remains its title.

The Coldstreamers have since proved themselves in battle over 350 years in conflicts around the world. They fought at the Battle of Waterloo in 1815, where it held the Château d'Hougoumont. In the Crimean War, four of the regiment's soldiers were awarded the newly instituted Victoria Cross.

The modern Coldstreamers serve as a light role infantry battalion in 4 Light Brigade Combat Team. During the Covid-19 pandemic in 2020, the regiment was deployed around London to help run testing centres to help detect the virus.

In 2027, they are to convert to the security assistance force role, providing training to local forces around the world.

ABOVE: The Coldstream Guards regularly parade during state ceremonial events. (MOD/CROWN COPYRIGHT)

LEFT: Soldiers of the Coldstream Guards won four of the then new Victoria Crosses for valour during the Crimean War. (MOD/CROWN COPYRIGHT)

Coldstream Guards (CLDM GDS)		
Formed	1650	
Successor units at formation	Monck's Regiment of Foot/The Lord General's Regiment of Foot Guards	
Recruiting areas	National	
Regular Battalion		
Unit	**Role**	**Location**
1st Battalion	Light	Windsor

Scots Guards

THE SCOTS Guards traces its origins to the Marquis of Argyll's Royal Regiment, a unit raised in 1642 by Archibald Campbell, 1st Marquess of Argyll in response to the 1641 Irish Rebellion. After the restoration of Charles II, the Earl of Linlithgow received a commission in November 1660 to raise a regiment which was called The Scottish Regiment of Footguards. It fought at the 1690 Battle of the Boyne.

Over the next 350 years it served around the world, including at Battle of Waterloo in 1815 and the Crimean War.

The modern regiment sent its 2nd Battalion to fight in the Falkland's conflict in 1982 and took part in one of the British Army's last bayonet charges to capture Mount Tumbledown. The regiment served several tours in Northern Ireland in the 1980s and 1990s, when the current defence secretary Ben Wallace was one of its officers.

The regiment was reduced to one battalion after the 1992 defence review and the surviving 1st Battalion was re-roled into armoured infantry with the Warrior infantry fighting vehicle. It deployed to Iraq and Afghanistan between 2004 and 2013. It is now equipped with Mastiff mine protected vehicles as part of 7 Light Mechanised Brigade Combat Team. The battalion is on a rotation schedule to spend two years out of every six years deployed in Cyprus from its home garrison at Catterick. It will be heading to the Mediterranean in 2025.

Scots Guards (SG)		
Formed	1642	
Successor units at formation	Marquis of Argyll's Royal Regiment	
Recruiting areas	Scotland, or those with Scottish ancestors	
Regular Battalion		
Unit	**Role**	**Location**
1st Battalion	Heavy Protected Mobility	Catterick

Irish Guards

THE IRISH Guards are the second youngest regiment of the Foot Guards and were formed in 1900 on Queen Victoria's orders to honour Irishmen who fought in the Boer War. Its Guardsmen proudly call themselves 'the Micks'. The Irish Guards soon established a formidable fighting reputation, with its Guardsmen boasting six Victoria Cross recipients, four from World War One and two from World War Two.

In recent years, the regiment has seen duty in the Balkans, Iraq, and Afghanistan. It was the first British unit to enter Pristina in June 1999 as NATO forces moved into Kosovo and in March 2003 was part of the 7 Armoured Brigade as it helped capture the Iraqi city of Basra. The regiment served two tours of duty in Afghanistan. It has since deployed to Iraq as part of Operation Shader to train local forces to take on so-called Islamic State (IS) fighters.

The Irish Guards are now attached to the 11 Security Assistance Force Brigade in the specialist training role, but this means it has been reduced in strength. It will have this commitment until 2027 and then will revert to a light infantry role in 4 Light Brigade Combat Team.

Since 1902, the regimental mascot has been an Irish Wolfhound and they are the only Guards regiment permitted to have their mascot lead them on parade. Prince William, who was then colonel of the Irish Guards, wore the uniform of the Irish Guards at his wedding to Catherine Middleton in 2012.

ABOVE: Seamus, the regimental mascot of the Irish Guards had a starring role in King Charles III's coronation in May 2023. (MOD/CROWN COPYRIGHT)

LEFT: The Irish Guards served on the frontline in Afghanistan in 2011 and more recently have deployed to Iraq as part of the war against the so-called Islamic State (IS). (MOD/CROWN COPYRIGHT)

Irish Guards (IG)		
Formed	1900	
Recruiting areas	Northern Ireland, or those with Irish ancestors	
Regular Battalion		
Unit	**Role**	**Location**
1st Battalion	Security Force Assistance	Aldershot

Welsh Guards

THE MOST junior regiment of the Foot Guards was formed in 1915 at the height of World War One. Within weeks of the regiment's formation, it was deployed to France where it took part in the fighting on the Western Front until the end of the war.

After distinguished service with the Guards Armoured Division in World War Two, the Welsh Guards served around the world during the conflicts linked to Britain's retreat from its empire.

The 1st Battalion sailed with the task force to liberate the Falklands Islands in 1982. Tragedy struck when Argentinian aircraft bombed the landing ship RFA *Sir Galahad*, which had soldiers of the Welsh Guards embarked. There were high casualties, 48 dead, including 32 Welsh Guards. Many wounded suffered from horrendous burns, the best-known being Simon Weston, who later became well known as a charity campaigner for war veterans.

After service in Northern Ireland, the Balkans and Iraq, the regiment deployed to Afghanistan in 2009, where it spearheaded the Operation Panther's Claw offensive against a key Taliban stronghold. During the battle it suffered six fatalities, including its commanding officer, Lieutenant Colonel Rupert Thorneloe, who died when his vehicle was blown up by a roadside bomb. He was first the British Army commanding officer killed in action since Lt Col 'H' Jones of the Parachute Regiment during the 1982 Falklands conflict.

The regiment has since deployed to Iraq in 2020 as part of Operation Shader to train local forces to fight IS insurgents. It is now based at Windsor to participate in state ceremonial events.

Welsh Guards (WG)		
Formed	1915	
Recruiting areas	Wales, or those with Welsh ancestors	
Regular Battalion		
Unit	**Role**	**Location**
1st Battalion	Light /Public Duties	Windsor

London Guards & Public Duties Companies

RED COATED Guardsmen are the public face of the British Army at the many state ceremonial events in London. The six Foot Guards and two mounted regiments with a ceremonial role are known as the Household Division. The funeral of Queen Elizabeth II last September and the coronation of King Charles III in May this year, saw the Household Division on parade in strength in London and Windsor.

Staging world class ceremonial events is a full-time task and Headquarters London District is responsible for mounting them. From the iconic Horseguards building, the staff of London District plan the complex ceremonial schedule, marshal the required troops, and then conduct the events.

The ceremonial calendar comprises a mix of small scale, routine and large events that attract global attention. On a weekly basis, troops are paraded outside the royal palaces in London and Windsor. There are also guards of honour for visiting heads of state and government. Each

LEFT: State ceremonial events in London are conducted by dedicated units and personnel of the Household Division. (MOD/CROWN COPYRIGHT)

year there are also a number of major events, such as Trooping the Colour, which require hundreds of Guardsmen to be on parade.

The main units of the Household Division have operational roles in the wider British Army so several dedicated units and detachments have been set up just to take part in

ceremonial events. Foot Guard units provide the following units, which are all based at Wellington Barracks in central London:

- Nijmegen Company, Grenadier Guards
- Number 7 Company, Coldstream Guards

BELOW: Practice makes perfect. Rigorous inspection and meticulous planning ensure state ceremonial events go off with a hitch. (MOD/CROWN COPYRIGHT)

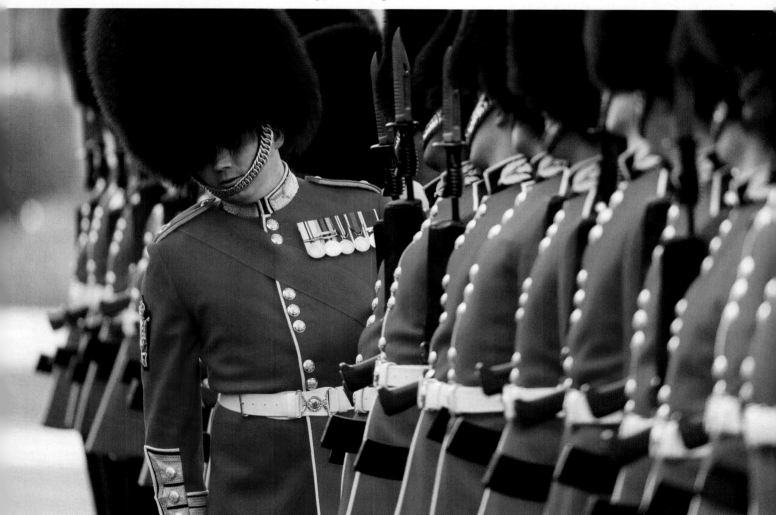

when terrorist threat levels are raised, as part of Operation Temperer.

In a new development in 2022, the London Regiment of the Army Reserve was renamed, the London Guards, and formally assigned to the Household Division to support operational and ceremonial tasks. The London Guards' companies were renamed as follows:

- HQ (London Irish Rifles) Company to become Number 15 (Loos) Company, Irish Guards.
- A (London Scottish) Company to become G (Messines) Company, Scots Guards.
- F (Rifles) Company to become Number 17 Company, Coldstream Guards.
- G (Guards) Company to become Ypres Company, Grenadier Guards

This is the first time the Foot Guards have been formally linked to the Army Reserve and many of the new regiment's officers and soldiers are former regular members of the Household Division.

- F Company, Scots Guards
- Number 9 Company, Irish Guards
- Number 12 Company, Irish Guards

The resident Foot Guards battalions at Windsor provide the public sentries at Windsor Castle.

Mounted detachments of the Life Guards and Blue & Royals are based at Hyde Park Barracks in London as part of the Household Cavalry Mounted Regiment. Ceremonial gun salutes are provided by the King's Troop of the Royal Horse Artillery, based at Woolwich.

To give the Foot Guards regiments a break from ceremonial duties to allow them to conduct important training, or operational tasks, other British Army regiments, the Royal Air Force Regiment and Commonwealth military contingents regularly take turns to provide troops for small scale ceremonial events, such as the Changing of the Guard outside Buckingham Palace.

As well as its ceremonial role, London District also has a secondary mission to provide military assistance to civil authorities, including armed support to the Metropolitan Police

London Guards (LONDON GDS)		
Formed	2022	
Successor units at formation	London Regiment	
Recruiting areas	London	
Reserve Battalion		
Unit	Role	Location
1st Battalion	Light /Ceremonial	London

Parachute Regiment

THE PARACHUTE Regiment is the British Army's elite airborne force. The three regular and one reserve battalion of the modern Parachute Regiment proudly maintain the traditions of their illustrious forebears, including wearing the famous maroon beret. Although one of the British Army's youngest regiments, it has established an unprecedented reputation for battle honours, including D-Day and Arnhem in World War Two and more recently it has seen action in the Falklands, Sierra Leone, Iraq, and Afghanistan,

Today, 2 and 3 PARA are the core of the British Army Global Response Force, 16 Air Assault Brigade Combat Team, with at least one battalion held at very high readiness to deploy to crisis zones at less than a day's notice.

This high readiness unit is known as the Air Manoeuvre Battlegroup 1, or AMBG 1, and at least one of its companies has to be ready to parachute into action. During the Sudan crisis in April 2023, 3 PARA was alerted to join the British non-combatant evacuation operation to bring UK passport holders to safety. The whole battalion was flown out to the British airbase on Cyprus and stood ready to parachute into Sudan to seize control of an airfield to allow RAF transport aircraft to bring out refugees. Fortunately, the security situation stabilised so the jump was not necessary. Paratroopers then provided security for RAF aircraft evacuating British passport holders from Port Sudan.

The Sudan mission followed on from 16 Brigade's central role in the August 2021 evacuation from the Afghan capital, Kabul. Operation Pitting saw nearly 15,000 Afghan refugees evacuated to safety in the UK.

LEFT: Paratroops of 2 PARA dropped in to North Norway in March 2023 to prove the British Army's airborne capability in arctic climates. (MOD/CROWN COPYRIGHT)

In addition to its commitment to conduct NEOs and short notice humanitarian operations, 16 Brigade has a wartime role carrying out rapid parachute and helicopter assaults behind enemy lines. Tactical air landing, or TALO, operations use RAF airlifters to deliver troops and vehicles into airfield or improvised air strips close to front line positions. This role was practiced during Exercise Swift Response in Macedonia in May 2022, when 2 PARA practised carrying out helicopter-borne air assault operations, supported by 105mm Light Guns of 7th Parachute Regiment Royal Horse Artillery and Army Air Corps Apache AH1 attack helicopters.

Since the 1960s, the main aircraft used by the Parachute Regiment ≫

LEFT: The Pathfinder Platoon of 16 Air Assault Brigade Combat Team using HALO parachuting techniques to covertly insert teams to mark drop zones for larger follow-up forces of paratroopers. (MOD/CROWN COPYRIGHT)

Parachute Regiment (PARA)

Formed	1942
Successor units at formation	Army Commandos, Special Air Service
Recruiting areas	National

Regular Battalions

Unit	Role	Location
1st Battalion (1 PARA)	Special Forces Support Group	St Athan
2nd Battalion (2 PARA)	Airborne	Colchester
3rd Battalion (3 PARA)	Airborne	Colchester

Reserve Battalion

Unit	Role	Location
4th Battalion (4 PARA)	Airborne	Pudsey

RIGHT: Paratroopers of 3 PARA are recognisable by the green DZ flash worn on their right shoulder. (MOD/CROWN COPYRIGHT)

has been the C-130 Hercules. These veteran aircraft were retired this June and the newer A400M Atlas is taking on the role as the main airdrop aircraft for the Parachute Regiment.

The Parachute Regiment also maintains strong links with its allied counterparts, including routinely jumping from their partner's troop-carrying aircraft to assess inter-operability.

Reserve paratroopers from 4 PARA are closely integrated with their regular counter-parts and are routinely called on to provide additional personnel, during major operational deployments or exercises.

The regiment's 1st Battalion is permanently attached to the Special Forces, and it is based in South Wales. Personnel serve in 1 PARA on rotation from other units of the regiment. Within 16 Brigade, the Pathfinder Platoon is the elite reconnaissance force. It is equipped and trained to conduct High Altitude Low Opening (HALO) parachute drops for covert insertions into enemy territory.

BELOW: In December 2022, 2 PARA deployed to Morocco for desert warfare training with the North African country's army. (MOD/CROWN COPYRIGHT)

Royal Irish Regiment (27th (Inniskilling), 83rd, 87th and Ulster Defence Regiment)

LEFT: Royal Irish soldiers parade in their distinctive green caubeen berets, which, in the British Army are now worn only by soldiers of the regiment. Irish linked regiments in Commonwealth armies also wear the caubeen and Irish Defence Force pipers wear black caubeens. (MOD/CROWN COPYRIGHT)

THE PROUD traditions of the British Army's Irish regiments are maintained by the modern Royal Irish Regiment. Its regular battalion serves as part of 16 Air Assault Brigade Combat Team, which is designated Britain's Global Response Force. Royal Irish soldiers continue to wear the traditional Irish beret known as the caubeen, with a green hackle.

1 R Irish was assigned to 16 Brigade on its formation in 1999 and it played a prominent part in British interventions in Sierra Leone, Afghanistan, and Iraq over the following decade. Since 2003, 12 members of the regiment have been awarded the Conspicuous Gallantry Cross or the Military Cross, the British Army's second and third most prestigious medals, respectively, for gallantry in Iraq and Afghanistan.

Its current role is to provide 16 Brigade with a light strike capability, operating in heavily armed Land Rovers and other vehicles.

In 2022, the battalion deployed to Mali to provide the United Nations force in the African country with a long-range desert patrol capability. During April and May 2023, the battalion practiced its light strike role on Salisbury Plain in co-operation with the Royal Gurkha Rifles and a contingent of troops from the Indian Army. The Royal Irish deployed by air in RAF A400M Atlas aircraft and Chinook transport helicopters.

BELOW: The Royal Irish Regiment played a prominent role in the 2003 invasion of Iraq where it captured many of the country's oil fields. (MOD/CROWN COPYRIGHT)

Royal Irish Regiment (R IRISH)		
Formed	1992	
Successor units at formation	Royal Irish Rangers, Ulster Defence Regiment	
Recruiting areas	Ireland, or those with Irish ancestors	
Regular Battalion		
Unit	Role	Location
1st Battalion (1 R IRISH)	Light Strike	Ternhill
Reserve Battalion		
Unit	Role	Location
2nd Battalion (2 R IRISH)	Light	Lisburn

Royal Regiment of Scotland

SCOTLAND'S HISTORIC infantry regiments are now part of the Royal Regiment of Scotland, which was formed in 2006 as part of a major overhaul of the British Army's structure. This 'super regiment' now comprises three regular battalions, a ceremonial unit and a two reserve battalions, as well as being affiliated to a battalion of the newly formed Ranger Regiment.

Few military organisations can rival the record for battlefield success, individual heroism, and sacrifice of Scotland's infantry regiments. The oldest antecedent unit of the Royal Regiment of Scotland is the Royal Scots. It was once known as the Royal Regiment of Foot, and is the oldest and most senior infantry regiment of the line of the British Army, having been raised in 1633 during the reign of Charles I. Then there is iconic Black Watch which can trace its history back to the Jacobite rebellions in 1725. Scottish soldiers have served in all of Britain's wars up to the modern era and their exploits are legendary.

Since its formation, the battalions of the Royal Regiment of Scotland have fought in Iraq and Afghanistan, as well serving on NATO duty in eastern Europe and peacekeeping missions around the globe. In June 2021, 3 SCOTS, the successors of the Black Watch were the final British Army regiment to be garrisoned in the Afghan capital, Kabul, and lowered the flag on 20 years of British military presence in the country.

The modern battalions of the Royal Regiment of Scotland have

very different roles. The 2nd Battalion has a light protected mobility role, using the Foxhound mine protected vehicle and is part of 4 Light Brigade Combat Team.

Advising and assisting local forces is the job of the 3 SCOTS, which is part of 11 Security Force Assistance Brigade.

Mastiff mine protected vehicles are used by 4 SCOTS in its heavy protected role with 7 Light Mechanised Brigade Combat Team. It dispatched troops to train with NATO forces in Estonia in May 2023 and during 2024 will be part of the NATO Very High Readiness Joint Task Force. The battalion is to spend two years in Cyprus from 2025.

Balaklava Company of 5 SCOTS has a public duties role in Edinburgh and played a central role in the ceremonial events during Queen Elizabeth II's lying in state in Edinburgh's St Giles Cathedral. The regiment's most high-profile officer during the events leading up to her funeral and at

The King's coronation in May 2003 was Major Johnny Thompson who was seen at King Charles III's side fulfilling his duties as the monarch's equerry.

To maintain the traditions of Scottish military music the regiment has its own marching band, and the battalions have their own pipe bands.

The two reserve battalions, 6 and 7 SCOTS, routinely mobilise personnel to serve in the regular battalions on exercises and operations.

In 2021, 1 SCOTS was converted into the 2nd Battalion, The Ranger Regiment, with the mission of training local forces in conflict zones. It continues to draw its personnel from the Royal Regiment of Scotland on temporary detachment.

ABOVE: The Royal Regiment of Scotland also recruits from across the Commonwealth. (MOD/CROWN COPYRIGHT)

LEFT: 4 SCOTS is to be part of the NATO Very High Readiness Task Force in 2024. (MOD/CROWN COPYRIGHT)

Royal Regiment of Scotland (SCOTS)

Formed	2006
Successor units at formation	Royal Scots, King's Own Scottish Borderers, Royal Highland Fusiliers, Black Watch, The Highlanders, Argyll and Sutherland Highlanders
Recruiting areas	Scotland, or those with Scottish ancestors

Regular Battalions

Unit	Role	Location
2nd Battalion (2 SCOTS)	Light Protected Mobility	Edinburgh
3rd Battalion (3 SCOTS)	Security Force Assistance	Fort George
4th Battalion (4 SCOTS)	Heavy Protected Mobility	Catterick
5th Battalion (5 SCOTS)	Public Duties	Edinburgh

Reserve Battalions

Unit	Role	Location
6th Battalion (6 SCOTS)	Light	Glasgow
7th Battalion (7 SCOTS)	Light	Perth

Royal Yorkshire Regiment
(14th/15th, 19th and 33rd/76th Foot)

THE ROYAL Yorkshire Regiment draws on the traditions of the county's historic infantry regiments that can trace their roots as far back as 1685. Its antecedent regiments fought in all of Britain's wars in the past 300 years until they were combined into the current regiment in 2007.

The Green Howards was formed during the 1688 'Glorious Revolution' from independent companies raised in Somerset to support William III. They picked up their famous nickname in 1744 during the War of the Austrian Succession under the command of Colonel Charles Howard. To differentiate them from another regiment commanded by a different Colonel Howard, they became the Green Howards on account of the green cuffs on their tunics.

The 33rd of Foot was commanded by Arthur Wellesley in India and subsequently became the famous Duke of Wellington's Regiment after the victor of the Battle of Waterloo was ennobled.

The West Yorkshire and East Yorkshire Regiments can both trace their history back to 1685 and eventually were merged to form the Prince of Wales's Own Regiment of Yorkshire in 1958.

Since the formation of the current 'super regiment', Yorkshire infantry soldiers have served extensively in Iraq and Afghanistan. A company-

sized contingent from 2 YORKS flew to Kabul in August 2021 to take part in Operation Pitting, to secure the evacuation of more than 15,000 refugees after Afghanistan fell to the Taliban.

Over the past 15 years the regiment has undergone considerable change as a result of a series of defence reviews. It was originally formed with three full infantry battalions, and it remained in this form until 2014 when the third battalion was disbanded. In its new form, the 1st Battalion was in the armoured infantry role, equipped with the Warrior infantry fighting vehicle. It deployed to Estonia in 2018 on NATO enhanced forward presence duty. The 2nd Battalion was in the light infantry role and deployed to Cyprus as the regional stand-by battalion.

The 2021 Integrated Review set in train a further reorganisation. This saw the 1st Battalion lose its Warriors and it converted to the

Royal Yorkshire Regiment (R YORKS)

Formed	2007
Successor units at formation	Green Howards, Duke of Wellington's Regiment, Prince of Wales's Own Regiment of Yorkshire
Recruiting areas	Yorkshire and Northeast

Regular Battalions

Unit	Role	Location
1st Battalion (1 R YORKS)	Light Protected Mobility	Catterick
2nd Battalion (2 R YORKS)	Experimental	Chester

Reserve Battalion

Unit	Role	Location
4th Battalion (4 R YORKS)	Light	York

light protected mobility role with the Foxhound mine protected vehicle. At the same time, the 2nd Battalion was converted to the British Army's experimental battalion to trial new tactics and equipment. In this new role, the size of the battalion is to be reduced to just over 200 soldiers.

On April 6, 2023, The Yorkshire Regiment was granted Royal status with immediate effect by King Charles III, changing the regiment's name to the 'Royal Yorkshire Regiment'. Soldiers of 1 R YORKS deployed to Northern Iraq in 2023 to participate in Operation Shader, the on-going mission to contain fighters of the so-called Islamic State group. The battalion is expected to be based in Cyprus for two years later in the decade.

LEFT: Soldiers of 2 R YORKS played an important role in the evacuation of refugees from Kabul in August 2021. (MOD/CROWN COPYRIGHT)

BELOW: Infantry soldiering is the bread and butter work of the Royal Yorkshire Regiment's two battalions. (MOD/CROWN COPYRIGHT)

Royal Welsh

ABOVE: The Royal Welsh are one of the British Army's four armoured infantry battalions, operating the battle proven Warrior vehicle, which boasts a 30mm Rarden cannon. (MOD/CROWN COPYRIGHT)

THE PRINCIPALITY'S infantry regiment has a long and distinguished history, stretching back to 1689 when one of its first antecedent units, the Royal Welch Fusiliers was formed. The Royal Welsh Regiment's most famous antecedent unit is the 24th Regiment of Foot, which was almost wiped out at the Battle of Isandlwana, in South Africa, in January 1879. A surviving detachment of 141 soldiers then fought off a large Zulu army of 4,000 fighters during the Battle of Rorke's Drift in an engagement that has been immortalised in the 1964 film *Zulu*. Eleven participants in the battle,

RIGHT: Infantry combat skills are put to the test by a Royal Welsh soldier during a NATO exercise in Estonia. (MOD/CROWN COPYRIGHT)

including seven from the 24th Foot, were awarded the Victoria Cross for their heroism.

In modern time, the Royal Welch Fusiliers served with distinction while besieged in the Bosnian town of Gorazde in 1995. After its formation, The Royal Welsh deployed on operations to Iraq and Afghanistan. In 2014, the regiment was downsized to two regular battalions, supported by its 3rd Battalion in the Army Reserve.

The current 1st Battalion is one of the British Army's four armoured infantry battalions, equipped with the Warrior infantry fighting vehicle, as part of 12 Armoured Brigade Combat Team. In this role it has deployed twice to Estonia since 2017 to function as the NATO enhanced forward presence battlegroup in the Baltic state. The regiment is to re-equip with the wheeled Boxer armoured personnel carrier later this decade.

Royal Welsh (R WELSH)		
Formed	2006	
Successor units at formation	Royal Welch Fusiliers, Royal Regiment of Wales	
Recruiting areas	Wales, or those with Welsh ancestors	
Regular Battalion		
Unit	Role	Location
1st Battalion (1 R WELSH)	Armoured	Tidworth
Reserve Battalion		
Unit	Role	Location
2nd Battalion (2 R WELSH)	Light	Cardiff

Princess of Wales's Royal Regiment (Queen's and Royal Hampshires)

THE REGIMENT is the most senior English line infantry regiment and the second most senior in British Army, after the Royal Scots. It can trace its history back to October 1661 when the Tangier Regiment, later to be known as the 2nd Regiment of Foot and the Queen's Royal Regiment, was first paraded on Putney Heath. It has the distinction of holding the earliest battle honour of the British Army, Tangier 1662–80.

The modern regiment came into existence in 1992 as a result of the post-Cold War defence cuts, which reduced the strength of the British Army by nearly 20%. Its name is derived from Diana, Princess of Wales, who was its first colonel-in-chief.

The 1st Battalion was formed as an armoured infantry battalion, equipped with the Warrior infantry fighting vehicle, and based in Germany. The 2nd Battalion was a light role infantry battalion based in Cyprus or in English garrisons.

In 2004, 1 PWRR was deployed to Al Amarah in southern Iraq and spent most of its tour fighting against insurgents around the city. During these battles, Private Johnson Beharry won the Victoria Cross, the first awarded since the 1982 Falklands conflict. The battalion returned to Iraq in 2006 and then served in Afghanistan in 2009 and 2011.

By 2018, both battalions were back in Britain for the first time since the formation of the regiment. In 2021, 2 PWRR moved out of the regiment and became the 2nd Battalion, The Ranger Regiment. The 1st Battalion is to convert to using the Boxer armoured personnel carrier in 2025.

BELOW: Private Johnson Beharry is the most famous member of the regiment after he won the Victoria Cross in Iraq in 2004 for rescuing his comrades from an insurgent ambush. (MOD/CROWN COPYRIGHT)

Princess of Wales's Royal Regiment (PWRR)		
Formed	1992	
Successor units at formation	Queen's Regiment, Royal Hampshire Regiment	
Recruiting areas	London, South East of England	
Regular Battalion		
Unit	**Role**	**Location**
1st Battalion (1 PWRR)	Light	Cyprus
Reserve Battalions		
Unit	**Role**	**Location**
3rd Battalion (3 PWRR)	Light	Canterbury
4th Battalion (4 PWRR)	Light	Redhill

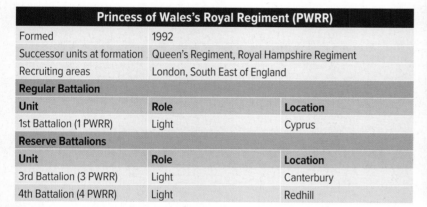

81mm Mortars provide support during a live fire exercise on Salisbury Plain by 1 PWRR. (MOD/CROWN COPYRIGHT)

Royal Anglian Regiment

RIGHT: Royal Anglian regiment soldiers fought a series of tough battles in Helmand province against the Taliban in 2007. (MOD/CROWN COPYRIGHT)

THE CURRENT Royal Anglian Regiment was formed in 1964 and has remained in continuous existence since then. making it the oldest of the line infantry regiment of the British Army of the modern era. Its antecedent regiments can trace their history back to 1685.

The regiment's badge consists of a silver star of eight points, upon which is the castle of Gibraltar with a scroll inscribed 'ROYAL ANGLIAN' in gold. This honours the Suffolk, Essex and Northamptonshire Regiments which all served during the Great Siege of Gibraltar from 1779 to 1783.

It was first of the British Army's 'large' or 'super' infantry regiments, comprising four regular and three Territorial Army battalions on its formation. This was a new initiative

BELOW: The 2nd Battalion travelled to Estonia in May 2023 to take part in NATO exercises in the Baltic state. (MOD/CROWN COPYRIGHT)

at the time and saw the regiment have battalions in different roles, allowing officers and soldiers to move around between units to gain experience and promotions.

Over the past five decades the regiment has undergone several reorganisations, as a result of a series defence reviews. It lost one regular battalion in 1975 and then in 1992 another regular and two Territorial battalions were disbanded. Each of the remaining battalions has its own nickname - the 1st Battalion is known as the Vikings; the 2nd Battalion are the Poachers; and the reservists of the 3rd Battalion are the Steelbacks.

Since the reorganisation, the regular battalions have seen extensive actions in several conflict zones. Both regular battalions deployed with the UN peacekeeping force in Bosnia in 1994 and 1995.

The 1st Battalion was one of the first units to deploy to Afghanistan after the fall of the Taliban in March 2002 at the start of the NATO peacekeeping mission in the central Asian country. It returned to Afghanistan five years later as part of the British move into Helmand province and for six months was locked in intense fighting with Taliban insurgents. The 1st Battalion returned to Helmand in 2009 and 2012 for further combat deployments.

Today, the 1st Battalion is based on Cyprus providing security for the British sovereign base areas and a small detachment of its soldiers is also based in Bahrain in the Arabian Gulf to protect the Royal Navy base there. In April 2023, the battalion was mobilised to set up a reception centre for refugees being evacuated from Sudan on Royal Air Force aircraft. It is to return to Britain in August 2023 and be based alongside the 2nd Battalion at Cottesmore in Rutland.

The 2nd Battalion is based at Cottesmore as part of 7 Light Mechanised Brigade Combat Team in the light infantry role. Soldiers from the regiment joined the United Nations peacekeeping force in Mali between 2020 and 2021. It has sent a company of soldiers in Foxhound mine protected vehicles to Estonia to join NATO exercises. During 2024, the battalion is to be part of the NATO Very High Readiness Joint Task Force.

The Royal Anglian Regiment has links to the Royal Bermuda Regiment (RBR) and provides a team of personnel to train the unit.

Royal Anglian Regiment (1 R ANGLIAN)		
Formed	1964	
Successor units at formation	1st East Anglian Regiment, 2nd East Anglian Regiment, 3rd East Anglian Regiment, Royal Leicestershire Regiment	
Recruiting areas	East of England	
Regular Battalions		
Unit	**Role**	**Location**
1st Battalion (1 R ANGLIAN)	Security Force Assistance	Cyprus
2nd Battalion (2 R ANGLIAN)	Light	Cottesmore
Reserve Battalion		
Unit	**Role**	**Location**
3rd Battalion (3 R ANGLIAN)	Light	Bury St Edmonds

BELOW: In 2022 the 2nd Battalion took part in NATO exercises in Norway to evaluate alliance defences in the high north. (MOD/CROWN COPYRIGHT)

Royal Regiment of Fusiliers

THE ORIGINAL fusiliers in the British Army were armed with an early version of flintlock weapons called a fusil, derived from the French word for the weapon. The 7th Foot, Royal Regiment of Fuzileers were first raised in 1685 and they were soon followed by other regiments of fusiliers. Many of these regiments also wore the distinctive mitre hat.

Modern fusiliers maintain their traditions by wearing a red and white hackle on their beret. Its other rank soldiers are still known as fusiliers, rather than privates.

Over the centuries, the fusiliers have established a reputation for bravery and earned numerous battle honours. During the 1915 Gallipoli landings the Lancashire Fusiliers famously won six Victoria Crosses in the space of a few hours 'before breakfast'.

The modern day 1st Battalion is known as the First Fusiliers and is one of the British Army's four armoured infantry battalions, equipped with the Warrior infantry fighting vehicle. It continues to serve with the Salisbury Plain–based 20 Armoured Brigade Combat Team.

Over the past 20 years, the First Fusiliers have seen action in Iraq, leading the 7 Armoured Brigade into action around the city of Basra. In recent years, the battalion deployed to Estonia in 2020 as part of NATO's enhanced forward presence. It is scheduled to return to Estonia later in 2023.

From 2025, the First Fusiliers are to be re-equipped with the Boxer wheeled armoured personnel carrier to boost their battlefield mobility.

Royal Regiment of Fusiliers (RRF)		
Formed	1968	
Successor units at formation	Royal Northumberland Fusiliers, Royal Warwickshire Fusiliers, Royal Fusiliers (City of London Regiment), Lancashire Fusiliers	
Recruiting areas	London, North East, Lancashire, Midlands	
Regular Battalion		
Unit	**Role**	**Location**
1st Battalion (1 RRF)	Armoured	Tidworth
Reserve Battalion		
Unit	**Role**	**Location**
5th Battalion (5 RRF)	Light	Newcastle

BELOW: First and foremost, the First Fusiliers are infantry soldiers. The regiment sent soldiers to wars in Iraq and Afghanistan, as well as conducting routine training around world, including here in the Falkland Islands. (MOD/CROWN COPYRIGHT)

Royal Gibraltar Regiment

IN 1704, Anglo-Dutch forces captured Gibraltar from Spain during the War of the Spanish Succession. The territory was ceded in perpetuity under the Treaty of Utrecht in 1713 and since then it has been Britain's strategic base at the western entrance to the Mediterranean. Local personnel have been recruited to help the British garrison defend the territory since 1710.

In 1938 the successor unit of the current Royal Gibraltar Regiment was formed as part of what was then the Territorial Army. These were civilians who trained at weekends to be ready to be mobilised in time of crisis or war. This tradition continues to this day with the regiment being made up of a permanent cadre of full-time soldiers, supported by reservists in emergencies.

The Gibraltar Defence Force was mobilised in 1939 to protect 'The Rock's' naval base and its anti-aircraft gunners shot down several German and Italian aircraft. It became the Royal Gibraltar Regiment in 1958. In 1991, Gibraltar's resident regular infantry battalion was withdrawn, and the Royal Gibraltar Regiment became the only permanent British Army unit based in the territory, with one of its three infantry companies being made up of reservists.

In recent years, the regiment has taken on an important role providing defence engagement with friendly nations in North Africa as they deal with political instability, terrorism, and refugee movements. It has sent detachments to train in Morocco and Gambia. The regiment also regularly sends detachments to train in the UK and its officers and specialists are trained in British Army training establishments in Britain.

Royal Gibraltar Regiment		
Formed	1958	
Successor units at formation	Gibraltar Defence Force	
Recruiting areas	Gibraltar	
Regular Battalion		
Unit	Role	Location
Royal Gibraltar	Light	Gibraltar

BELOW: The Royal Gibraltar Regiments shows its respects to Queen Elizabeth II. Its gun detachment has just fired a salute to the passed monarch. (MOD/CROWN COPYRIGHT)

Mercian Regiment
(Cheshires, Worcesters and Foresters, and Staffords)

RIGHT: A Mercian soldier participating in an exercise in Sweden in June 2023 to bolster the Scandinavian country's bid to join NATO. (MOD/CROWN COPYRIGHT)

THE MERCIAN Regiment has taken on the traditions of several of the British Army's most famous county infantry regiments and is known as 'The Heart of England's Infantry'. The regiment's cap badge is a double headed Mercian Eagle with Saxon crown. It has also inherited the Swaledale ram mascot of the former Worcestershire and Sherwood Foresters Regiment, the glider shoulder flash of the Staffordshire regiment, and the oak leaves and acorn collar badges from the Cheshire Regiment.

It was originally formed in 2007 with three battalions and it has since been progressively reduced in size. A battalion was lost in 2014 and as a result of the 2021 Integrated Review, the regiment's 2nd Battalion was disbanded, and its personnel transferred to 1 MERCIAN or other units.

In the years after its formation, the Mercian battalions were heavily committed to operations in Iraq and Afghanistan. 1 MERCIAN deployed once to Iraq in 2008 in the final years of the British presence in the Middle East country. From 2007 to 2013, the regiment's battalions deployed to Afghanistan on six occasions.

The modern 1st Battalion is one of the British Army's four armoured infantry battalions, equipped with the Warrior infantry fighting vehicle. It continues to serve with the Salisbury Plain–based 12 Armoured Brigade Combat Team.

In recent years, 1 MERCIAN has deployed to Estonia as part of the British armoured battlegroup providing NATO's enhanced forward presence in the Baltic state.

BELOW: Warrior infantry fighting vehicles of the Mercian regiment on the move in Sweden during joint exercises in June 2023. (MOD/CROWN COPYRIGHT)

Mercian Regiment (MERCIAN)		
Formed	2007	
Successor units at formation	Cheshire Regiment, Staffordshire Regiment, Worcestershire and Sherwood Foresters Regiment	
Recruiting areas	West & East Midlands, Cheshire	
Regular Battalion		
Unit	**Role**	**Location**
1st Battalion (1 MERCIAN)	Armoured	Bulford
Reserve Battalion		
Unit	**Role**	**Location**
4th Battalion (4 MERCIAN)	Light	Wolverhampton

Duke of Lancaster's Regiment
(King's, Lancashire, and Border)

In April 2023, Kingsmen of the Duke of Lancaster's Regiment flew to Sudan to help in the evacuation of the UK passport holders from the war torn African country. (MOD/CROWN COPYRIGHT)

THE NORTHWEST of England's infantry regiment was formed in 2006 and has since regularly been deployed on operations to Iraq and Afghanistan. It is nicknamed the 'Lions of England' after its distinctive collar badge inherited from the King's Own Royal Regiment and this is now used on the current regimental tactical recognition flash. Its other rank soldiers are known as Kingsmen, rather than privates.

1 LANCS is now a light role infantry battalion, and it is based on the British sovereign base area on the island of Cyprus. It is currently the regional standby battalion, and its troops are held at high readiness to deploy at short notice to crisis zones. In April,

soldiers from 1 LANCS deployed to Sudan to assist with the evacuation of British passport holders from the war-torn country.

The regiment's reserve battalion regularly contributes to operational missions, including mobilising a company of soldiers for a six month tour of duty with the United Nations peacekeeping force on Cyprus in 2016. In 2023, 4 LANCS was mobilised to provide instructors to train Ukrainian soldiers at bases around Britain under the banner of Operational Interfex.

In December 2021, the regiment's 2nd Battalion was re-badged as the 3rd Battalion, The Ranger Regiment, with the mission to train local forces in crisis zones.

From its base on Cyprus Kingsmen of the Duke of Lancaster's Regiment conduct training across the Middle East, including here in Jordan. (MOD/CROWN COPYRIGHT)

Duke of Lancaster's Regiment (LANCS)		
Formed	2006	
Successor units at formation	King's Own Royal Border Regiment, King's Regiment, Queen's Lancashire Regiment	
Recruiting areas	Northwest, Isle of Man	
Regular Battalion		
Unit	**Role**	**Location**
1st Battalion (1 LANCS)	Light	Cyprus
Reserve Battalion		
Unit	**Role**	**Location**
4th Battalion (4 LANCS)	Light	Preston

Royal Gurkha Rifles

THE BRITISH Army's Gurkha soldiers have a reputation for bravery and loyalty in battle that stretches back more than 200 years. They are closely associated with the kukri, a forward-curving knife, which by reputation can only be unsheathed if it is going to be used to draw blood.

Gurkha soldiers were first encountered in the Anglo-Nepalese war and the British were so impressed by the fighting qualities of their opponents that after the signing of the Treaty of Sugauli in 1816, they started recruiting Gurkhas into the British-led Indian Army.

In the ensuing centuries, Gurkha battalions have proved themselves in battle on countless occasions and soldiers from Gurkha regiments have been awarded 26 Victoria Crosses, Britain's highest award for battlefield gallantry. The last was awarded in 1966 during Britain's confrontation with Indonesia. Half of the VCs were made to British officers in Gurkha units, which is testimony to the strong bond that exists within the unique force.

In 1947, Britain gave India its independence and this resulted in the so-called Tripartite Treaty that split the Gurkha troops between the new Indian army, the British Army and Nepal. This gave Britain the right to recruit Gurkhas soldiers and set many of their terms of conditions of service.

Today, just over 4,000 Gurkhas serve in the British Army and around half of them serve in the main infantry unit of the Brigade of Gurkhas, the Royal Gurkha Rifles (RGR). The remainder serve in Gurkha engineer, logistics and signals units. Competition to serve in the British

Royal Gurkha Rifles (RGR)		
Formed	1994	
Successor units at formation	2nd King Edward VII's Own Gurkha Rifles, 6th Queen Elizabeth's Own Gurkha Rifles, 7th Duke of Edinburgh's Own Gurkha Rifles, 10th Princess Mary's Own Gurkha Rifles	
Recruiting areas	Nepal	
Regular Battalions		
Unit	Role	Location
1st Battalion (1 RGR)	Air Assault	Brunei
2nd Battalion (2 RGR)	Light	Folkstone

Army is fierce with 20,000 applicants trying their hand to win one of just 204 places in 2023.

Modern Gurkhas serve around the world. The RGR saw extensive service in Afghanistan during British combat operations in country from 2006 to 2014.

One of the RGR's two infantry battalions is home based in Brunei as part of a long established arrangement with the country's Sultan. It is the only British military unit permanently based in the Far East and helps to run the British Army's jungle training unit in the country. In 1999, the Brunei-based battalion spearheaded the British intervention in East Timor and earlier in 2023 conducted joint training with the US Marine Corps and Australian Defence Forces around Darwin in Northern Australia.

The UK-based RGR battalion is garrisoned in Folkstone and is assigned to 16 Air Assault Brigade Combat Team, in the air assault role. This battalion is at high readiness to deploy around the world at short notice and 1 RGR practiced this role in a major exercise on Salisbury Plain in May 2023, in co-operation with a unit of the Indian Army.

In 2016, plans were announced to form a third RGR battalion, in what was then called the specialist infantry role, to provide advice and training to local forces in combat zones. This role has since passed to the recently formed Ranger Regiment. Two companies of Gurkhas are now attached to the Ranger Regiment.

LEFT: During May 2023, Gurkha soldiers deployed to Darwin to train with the Australian Army and US Marines. (MOD/CROWN COPYRIGHT)

BELOW: 2 RGR is currently part of 16 Air Assault Brigade Combat Team and is held at high readiness for rapid reaction missions around the world. (MOD/CROWN COPYRIGHT)

The Rifles

THE BRITISH Army's largest infantry regiment traces its roots back to the famous Light Division of the Napoleonic wars, incorporating many of the iconic regiments from that era. The Riflemen and Light Infantry of Sir John Moore's divisions were trained to operate in small teams ahead of the 'thin red line' of the British Army, picking off enemy commanders with well aimed rifle fire or scouting out weak points in enemy defences.

The modern Rifles incorporate many traditions from this era, including the bugle horn cap badge of Light Infantry and it marches at double pace to its regimental march. Its private soldiers are known as Riflemen and sergeants are titled Serjeant. Uniquely, Riflemen sport two beret badges. In addition to the bugle horn, they also wear the Egypt badge of the Gloucestershire Regiment on the back of their berets. This is in honour of the 28th Foot who famously formed a line facing both front and back when surrounded at the Battle of Alexandria in 1801.

It was formed as one of the new 'super' infantry regiments in 2007 with five regular and three Territorial

Army or reserve battalions. The amalgamation took place when one of the regiment's battalions was deployed on operations in Iraq and over the next seven years several of its units deployed to Afghanistan. It was engaged in tough fighting during Operation Panthers Claw in 2009 and then in Sangin.

After the British Army withdrew from combat operations in Helmand province in 2014, Rifles battalions

have since been regularly deployed to new hot spots. The 1st Battalion was the first British unit to begin training Iraqi and Kurdish troops in 2015 to fight off the advance of so-called Islamic State (IS) fighters. Two years later, the 2nd Battalion returned to Iraq to continue this mission.

In 2017, the 5th Battalion was the first British infantry battalion to deploy to Estonia to set up NATO's enhanced forward presence in

the Baltic state. The 5th Battalion returned to Estonia in 2020 and in 2022 the 2nd Battalion operated across the Baltic states and Scandinavia as a helicopter-borne rapid reaction force. During this deployment, troops of the 2nd Battalion exercised for the first time in Finland, ahead of its bid to join NATO.

The regiment is unique in having four regular full strength infantry battalions. Three of these – the 1st, 2nd, and 3rd Battalions – are light role infantry units and the 5th Battalion is an armoured infantry battalion,

assigned to 20 Armoured Brigade Combat Team. The 1st Battalion is to deploy to the British sovereign bases on Cyprus in 2024, to be the regional standby reserve unit for the Middle East and Africa.

In 2021, the 4th Battalion was converted into the 4th Battalion, The Ranger Regiment, with the mission of training local forces in conflict zones. It continues to draw its personnel from the Rifles on temporary detachment.

Many Rifles officers rise to the top of the British Army and armed forces. These include the recent former chief of the defence staff, General Sir Nick Carter, and the current head of the army, General Sir Patrick Sander. The current Queen, Camilla, also has a strong association with the regiment. She has been colonel-in-chief since 2020 and before that was royal colonel of the 4th Battalion since its formation 2007.

ABOVE: The support weapons company of 3 RIFLES was detached to serve in Estonia for six months from March 2023. (MOD/CROWN COPYRIGHT)

BELOW: An 81mm mortar team of 2 RIFLES lays down fire support during an infantry live fire exercise in Kenya. (MOD/CROWN COPYRIGHT)

The Rifles (RIFLES)		
Formed	2007	
Successor units at formation	Light Infantry, Royal Green Jackets, Royal Gloucestershire, Berkshire and Wiltshire Regiment, Devonshire and Dorset Regiment	
Recruiting areas	Southwest, Midlands, Northeast, London, Home Counties, Yorkshire	
Regular Battalions		
Unit	**Role**	**Location**
1st Battalion (1 RIFLES)	Light	Chepstow
2nd Battalion (2 RIFLES)	Light Protected Mobility	Lisburn
3rd Battalion (3 RIFLES)	Security Assistance	Edinburgh
5th Battalion (5 RIFLES)	Armoured	Bulford
Reserve Battalions		
Unit	**Role**	**Location**
6th Battalion (6 RIFLES)	Light Infantry	Exeter
7th Battalion (7 RIFLES)	Light Infantry	Reading
8th Battalion (8 RIFLES)	Light Infantry	Bishop Auckland

The Ranger Regiment

In the Grey Zone

To counter so-called hybrid threats in situations short of all out war, the British Army has formed a unique regiment to specialise in operations in what has become known as the 'Grey Zone'.

In December 2021, the Ranger Regiment stood up and it took under its command the four specialist infantry battalions that previously had the role of training and advising allied armies or friendly militia groups.

Each of the Ranger Regiment's four battalions has a dedicated area of responsibility so personnel can build up language skills, local knowledge, and contacts with key local decision makers. Since the regiment's formations, Ranger personnel have deployed in several countries in the Middle East and Africa, as well as training the Ukrainian army on

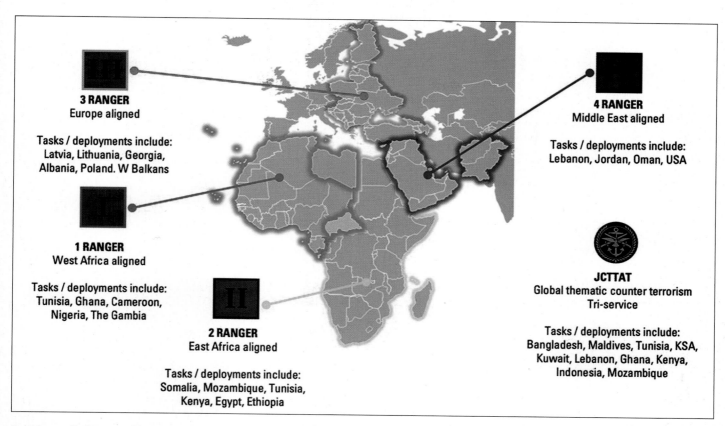

3 RANGER
Europe aligned

Tasks / deployments include:
Latvia, Lithuania, Georgia,
Albania, Poland. W Balkans

1 RANGER
West Africa aligned

Tasks / deployments include:
Tunisia, Ghana, Cameroon,
Nigeria, The Gambia

2 RANGER
East Africa aligned

Tasks / deployments include:
Somalia, Mozambique, Tunisia,
Kenya, Egypt, Ethiopia

4 RANGER
Middle East aligned

Tasks / deployments include:
Lebanon, Jordan, Oman, USA

JCTTAT
Global thematic counter terrorism
Tri-service

Tasks / deployments include:
Bangladesh, Maldives, Tunisia, KSA,
Kuwait, Lebanon, Ghana, Kenya,
Indonesia, Mozambique

British supplied anti-tank weapons in the days before the Russian invasion in February 2022.

The Ranger Regiment is assigned to the Army Special Operations Brigade, which was specially formed in August 2021 to take the lead on training partner nations, but also fights alongside them in 'complex high-threat environments'.

As well as the Ranger Regiment, the brigade also has two reinforcement companies of the Royal Gurkha Rifles, along with 255 Signal Squadron under command and 1 Squadron Honourable Artillery Company attached to provide long-range surveillance patrols.

For this unique role, these units are to be re-equipped with new weapons, uniforms, and other kit, under the Army Special Operations, Light Forces and Individual Combat Lethality and Protection project. This is budgeted at between £600m and £800m, according to the Ministry of Defence's Land Industrial Strategy. Around £120m will be spent on equipment for the Ranger Regiment alone over the next four years.

The first phase of this project involves the purchase of what is called the Alternative Individual Weapon (AIW) System. In tender documents issued to 16 international companies, this is to be a variant of the proven US 5.56mm calibre Armalite Rifle. This is required to have signature reduction systems and optics for close quarter battle, as well as a blank firing system. More than 1,000 weapons are required to equip the four Ranger battalions and delivery of the first rifles commenced in August 2022.

The Rangers are also looking to replace their standard issue UK Multi Terrain Pattern or MPT camouflage uniforms. The Crye MultiCam combat shirts and trousers have already been trialled by the Rangers and a bigger order is now expected.

There are few details of the other elements of the Army Special Operations, Light Forces and Individual Combat Lethality and Protection project but British Army sources suggest this could include new lightweight body armour, helmets, and boots.

ABOVE: The Ranger battalions are each aligned to a specific area of responsibility. (MOD/CROWN COPYRIGHT)

LEFT: Members of the Ranger Regiment took part in King Charles III's coronation ceremony and two of its young officers were photographed during the main rehearsal for the event. (MOD/CROWN COPYRIGHT)

The Ranger Regiment		
Unit	**Former Title**	**Location**
1st Battalion (1 Ranger)	1 SCOTS	Lisburn
2nd Battalion (2 Ranger)	2 PWRR	Ash Vale
3rd Battalion (3 Ranger)	2 LANCS	Pirbright
4th Battalion (4 Ranger)	4 RIFLES	Aldershot
G (Coriano) Company	3 RGR (att 4 Ranger)	Aldershot
F (Falklands) Company	3 RGR (att 2 Ranger)	Ash Vale

Special Forces

Who Dares Wins and More

The famous Special Air Service (SAS) Regiment has a global reputation that is second to none among the world's special forces units. It was formed in World War Two to take the fight behind enemy lines in North Africa and has since seen almost continuous service on counterinsurgency, counterterrorist and other operations that require its unique soldiers.

Over the past 20 years the UK Special Forces Group has grown into a significant organisation that involves multiple units and more than 3,000 personnel from the British Army, Royal Marines and Royal Air Force.

The army component of the special forces is mainly based at the home of the SAS at Stirling Lines in Credenhill, near Hereford. As well as the long-established 22 SAS Regiment, the base is home to the covert surveillance operatives of the

Special Forces Group Major Units, 2023		
Headquarters Special Forces Group	**Regent's Park, London**	
22 Special Air Service Regiment	Special Forces Operations	Stirling Lines, Credenhill
Special Reconnaissance Regiment	Surveillance Operations	Stirling Lines, Credenhill
1st Battalion, The Parachute Regiment (1 PARA)	Special Forces Support Group	RAF St Athan
Special Boat Service	Maritime Speical Forces Operations	RM Poole
7 Squadron, RAF	Chinook helicopters	RAF Odiham
658 Squadron, AAC	Dauphin helicopter	Credenhill

Special Reconnaissance Regiment (SRS) and specialist communications experts of 18 Signals Regiment. A detachment of the Army Air Corps, assigned to 658 Squadron AAC, is also based at Stirling Lines to rapidly deploy personnel on counter-terrorist operations around the UK.

Since 2004, the Parachute Regiment has provided a battalion of its highly trained soldiers to serve in the Special Forces Support Group (SFSG), based at RAF St Athan in South Wales. This unit is akin to the US Army Rangers and is trained and equipped to mount large-scale raids behind enemy lines or to seize forward operating bases for other units of the Special Forces.

To serve in the SAS or SRS, soldiers have to undergo a gruelling selection and training process. Only a small fraction of the volunteers pass and end up being 'badged' as fully fledged special forces operatives. There are two Army Reserve SAS units, 21 SAS (Artists Rifles) and 23 SAS Regiment, and potential recruits have to pass a version of the selection process to serve in them.

UK special forces are known to have been involved in almost every conflict in the British armed forces over the past 30 years, from the 1991 Gulf War to the recent conflict against so-called Islamic State (IS) in Syria and Iraq. There is close co-operation between US, Australian, and other allied special forces units.

The SAS really entered the public psyche after the 1980 Iranian Embassy rescue operation and since then the regiment and other elements of the special forces have provided specialist support to counter-terrorist police throughout the UK.

Special forces units are often equipped with specialist weapons, equipment, and vehicles for their unique role.

Most aspects of special forces are highly classified, and the Ministry of Defence routinely declines to comment their operations.

LEFT: In Afghanistan, the Special Forces Support Group operated in co-operation with the US Marines as part of Task Force 444.
(US DOD/COMBAT CAMERA)

BELOW: British special forces have their own squadron of Dauphin helicopters to move them to counterterrorist incidents around the UK.
(MARK HARKIN)

Royal Artillery

Close Support Artillery

FIRE SUPPORT for the British Army's two armoured brigade combat teams is provided the two regiments of Royal Artillery equipped with the AS90 155mm self-propelled gun.

The 1st Regiment Royal Horse Artillery (1 RHA) and 19 Regiment RA each have three gun batteries, which in turn each have eight AS90s. Their mission is to provide close fire support for armoured battlegroups, both in defence and attack. Royal Artillery forward observer officers, or FOOs, direct this fire from armoured vehicles operating as part of the armoured battlegroups. This fire is primary intended to hit enemy frontline positions, but the FOOs also have access to video feeds from unmanned aerial vehicles (UAVs) to allow them to strike at targets behind the enemy's frontline.

The AS90 was originally ordered in the late 1980s to replace the US-supplied M109 and M110 self propelled weapons that saw service in the 1991 Gulf War, as well as the British-designed 105mm Abbot. It was the first new British self-propelled gun to be fielded since the Abbot entered service in 1965.

The weapon incorporated digital gun-laying technology to speed the passage of targeting information from forward artillery observers. AS90 guns deployed on operations for the first time in 1996 when the Royal Artillery sent them to Bosnia as part of the NATO peacekeeping mission. The weapon first saw combat in March and April 2003, when AS90 batteries supported the advance by British Army troops from Kuwait to Basra. They then remained in the country to provide counter-battery fire for British troops under attack from insurgent mortars and rockets. An AS90 battery has been deployed on NATO duty in Estonia since 2017 as part of the British enhanced forward presence battlegroup.

As a result of the 2021 Integrated Review, the two AS90 regiments were grouped together as part of the new 1 Deep Strike Recce Brigade Combat Team. The two regiments are each to be augmented by a new battery of tactical groups, or Tac Groups, which are teams of specialist personnel who operate inside battlegroups headquarters directing artillery fire and monitoring video feeds from UAVs. Early in 2023, the British government donated 32 of the British Army's 89 AS90s to the Ukrainian army and the Royal Artillery ran a training programme for the gun's new owners.

BELOW: Ukrainian gunners travelled to Larkhill in early 2023 to learn how to operate the AS90s donated to them by the British government. (MOD/CROWN COPYRIGHT))

1st Regiment Royal Horse Artillery (1 RHA)

THE ROYAL Horse Artillery is a distinct arm of the Royal Regiment of Artillery and 1 RHA in turn is the most senior RHA unit. The regiment itself was formed in 1901 but its component batteries can trace their histories back to the Napoleonic and Revolutionary wars, with one battery being formed in 1793.

RIGHT: Royal Artillery AS90 crews live firing in Estonia in February 2023 as part of their NATO deployment. (MOD/CROWN COPYRIGHT)

1st Regiment Royal Horse Artillery (1 RHA)	
Formed	1901
Location	Larkhill
Equipment	AS90 155mm Self-Propelled Guns

19 Regiment RA

THE REGIMENT is known as the Scottish Gunners, because of its recruitment area in Scotland. It deployed to Bosnia in 1995 and fired its 105mm Light Guns to help lift the siege of Sarajevo. After being re-equipped with the AS90 in 1999, it fought in Iraq in 2005. It was temporarily re-equipped with 105mm Light Guns for a tour in Afghanistan in 2007.

19 Regiment RA	
Formed	1900
Location	Larkhill
Equipment	AS90 155mm Self-Propelled Guns

RIGHT: The business end of an AS90, as a 155mm shell is fired towards a target in Estonia by 127 Battery of 19 Regiment.
(MOD/CROWN COPYRIGHT)

104 Regiment RA

THIS ARMY Reserve regiment has the role of providing individual personnel to augment 1 RHA and 19 Regiment RA in time of war.

104 Regiment RA	
Formed	1967
Location	Newport
Equipment	AS90 155mm Self-Propelled Guns

RIGHT: The AS90 is highly mobile and able to keep up with the rapid advance of armoured battlegroups.
(MOD/CROWN COPYRIGHT)

Light Close Support Artillery

LIGHT INFANTRY, airborne and amphibious formations of the British Army and Royal Marines are supported by Royal Artillery regiments equipped with the 105mm Light Gun.

The classic 105mm Light Gun has seen action in many operations since it entered service more than 40 years ago. It is the only artillery system in British Army service that can be underslung beneath helicopters or air-dropped by parachute.

The 105mm Light Gun saw action for the first time in the 1982 Falklands conflict when batteries were flown forward by helicopter to support the final infantry assault on Port Stanley. Since then, Light Gun-equipped batteries have seen action in Bosnia, the 2003 Iraq war and in Afghanistan from 2006 to 2014.

Over the years, the 105mm Light Gun has been upgraded with new sights, but its simplicity and reliability are its hallmark. The weapon is one of the few 105mm class of field guns still in service around the world.

LEFT: In the summer of 2022, the Royal Artillery trained Ukrainian gunners to fire the 105mm Light Gun. (MOD/CROWN COPYRIGHT)

7th Parachute Regiment Royal Horse Artillery

7 RHA is the main fire support unit of 16 Air Assault Brigade Combat Team, and it is the only Royal Artillery unit trained and equipped to be delivered into battle by parachute. It has had the airborne role since 1966. It fired its guns in anger to support the Paratroopers of 16 Brigade in Iraq in 2003 and then in Afghanistan in 2006 and 2008. A battery is held at high readiness to deploy by air alongside the air manoeuvre battlegroup of the Parachute regiment.

7th Parachute Regiment Royal Horse Artillery (7 RHA)	
Formed	1961
Location	Colchester
Equipment	105mm Light Gun

LEFT: 7th Parachute Regiment Royal Horse Artillery live firing during a NATO exercise in Macedonia. (MOD/CROWN COPYRIGHT)

4 Regiment RA

4 REGIMENT RA is the fire support unit of 7 Light Mechanised Brigade Combat Team. It saw action in the Falklands war in 1982 as 5 Infantry's Brigade's 105mm Light Gun regiment, but soon afterwards moved to Germany to re-equip with self-propelled guns. It returned to Britain in 2008 and re-equipped with the 105mm Light Gun, deploying twice to Afghanistan between 2007 and 2008. During 2024 it is to be assigned to NATO's Very High Readiness Joint Task Force.

4 Regiment RA	
Formed	1939
Location	Topcliff
Equipment	105mm Light Gun

29 Commando Regiment RA

MEMBERS OF 29 Commando Regiment RA are all trained as Army Commandos to allow them to participate in amphibious operations as part of the Royal Marine's 3 Commando Brigade.

The regiment was assigned to 3 Commando Brigade in 1960 and since then it has supported the Royal Marines on all their major operations. It took the first British artillery ashore onto the Falkland Islands in 1982 and in 2003 was landed by helicopter on Iraq's al Faw Peninsular as part of the British amphibious operation to open the invasion of Iraq.

It supported 3 Commando Brigade on its three operational tours in Afghanistan between 2007 and 2011. Artillery observers from the regiment's 148 (Meiktila) Commando Forward Observation Battery are specially trained to direct naval gunfire support from Royal Navy and Allied warships. They were deployed to warships off the coast of Libya in 2011 to direct shore bombardments of the North African country's coastline.

29 Commando Regiment RA	
Formed	1947
Location	Plymouth
Equipment	105mm Light Gun

103 Regiment RA

The regiment is the main fire support unit attached to 4 Light Brigade Combat Team, and it is organised as a complete unit, with five gun batteries.

103 Regiment RA	
Formed	1859
Location	St Helens
Equipment	105mm Light Gun

105 Regiment RA

THE MAIN operational role of 105 Regiment RA is to augment its regular counterparts in 4 Regiment RA, as part of 7 Light Mechanised Brigade Combat Team. This involves providing the weapons and crews for the seventh and eighth gun in each of 4 Regiment RA's batteries.

105 Regiment RA	
Formed	1986
Location	Edinburgh
Equipment	105mm Light Gun

ABOVE: The 105mm Light Gun is the only artillery system used by the British armed forces that can be underslung by an RAF Chinook support helicopter.
(MOD/CROWN COPYRIGHT)

LEFT: 105mm Light Guns of the Army Reserve's 105 Regiment RA fire a salute for King Charles III on his coronation day in May 2023.
(MOD/CROWN COPYRIGHT)

Deep Fires

THE ROLE of the Royal Artillery's Multiple Launch Rocket System (MLRS) regiments is striking targets deep behind enemy lines. The US-designed MLRS weapon has been used by the Royal Artillery in the 1991 Gulf War, the 2003 invasion of Iraq and in Afghanistan from 2008.

The MLRS system is based on the M270 launcher vehicle, and it can fire a variety of weapons, with 12 rockets being fitted to the basic launcher. When it was introduced in the 1980s, the Royal Artillery used the original bomblet dispensing rocket but from 2008 it began using the Guided MLRS, or GLMRS, M31 rocket which has a range of up 91km and a single, unitary warhead.

In 2021 a major upgrade was started with the Royal Artillery's M270 launchers currently being modified to allow them to fire a portfolio of rockets, including the Guided MLRS Extended Range (GMLRS-ER) missile which will extend the army's reach out to 150km.

All the MLRS regiments are assigned to 1 Deep Strike Recce Brigade Combat Team. 3 RHA began converting to operate the MLRS in March 2023.

The two regular MLRS regiments each have two firing batteries and a tactical group, or tac group, battery to co-ordinate fire missions. The Army Reserve MLRS unit, 101 Regiment RA provides each of the regular MLRS regiments with a third battery, as well as individual personnel to augment them.

3rd Regiment Royal Horse Artillery (3 RHA)	
Formed	1938
Location	Newcastle
Equipment	Multiple Launch Rocket System (MLRS)

26 Regiment RA	
Formed	1947
Location	Larkhill
Equipment	Multiple Launch Rocket System (MLRS)

101 Regiment RA	
Formed	1860
Location	Newcastle
Equipment	Multiple Launch Rocket System (MLRS)

Surveillance Target Acquisition

FINDING TARGETS for the Royal Artillery's guns and rockets is the job of surveillance target acquisition units. A top priority is rapid detection of enemy artillery, rocket, and mortar systems so counter-battery fire can be directed against it to stop friendly forces taking casualties.

5 Regiment RA operates a number of target locating systems on behalf of 1 Deep Strike Recce Brigade Combat Team. Wide area surveillance is provided by the Saab Mobile Artillery Monitoring Battlefield Asset (MAMBA) weapon-locating radar systems, which have been in service since 2006 and can detect enemy shells or rockets in flight. Sound ranging technology is also used to detect enemy shells or rockets, via the Hostile Artillery LOcating (HALO) system. Enemy troops moving at night or in bad weather can be detected by the ground-mounted MSTAR radar system.

In some tactical situations it may be necessary to redeploy highly trained teams to hide in camouflaged observation posts for extended periods. 5 Regiment RA's 4/73 (Sphinx) Special Observation Post Battery provides these teams.

The Army Reserve's Honourable Artillery Company (HAC) provides a similar capability to the Army Special Operations Brigade. It was incorporated by royal charter in 1537 by King Henry VIII, making it the oldest regiment in the British Army.

BELOW: The MAMBA target locating radar allows the Royal Artillery to pinpoint enemy mortar and artillery firing positions within seconds of them opening fire. (MOD/CROWN COPYRIGHT)

5 Regiment RA	
Formed	1939
Location	Catterick
Equipment	MAMBA, MSTAR, HALO

Honourable Artillery Company (HAC)	
Formed	1537
Location	London
Equipment	105mm Light Gun for ceremonial events

Air Defence

SINCE 1998, the Royal Artillery has been the sole operator of air defence surface-to-air missiles (SAMs) in the UK armed forces. In 2019, the Royal Artillery's three air defence regiments were grouped together under the command of 7 Air Defence Group, based at Thorney Island in Sussex.

The Royal Artillery operates two types of air defence SAMs, the Sky Sabre area weapon, and the close range Starstreak High Velocity Missile (HVM).

Sky Sabre was ordered to replace the aging Rapier SAM system and the initial requirement was only to buy enough to replace the air defence network protecting the Falkland Islands, but the long term ambition is to field a deployable air defence capability to protect the British Army elsewhere in the world.

BELOW: Sky Sabre is the Royal Artillery's new air defence system, and it has been deployed in Poland and the Falklands since early 2022.
(MOD/CROWN COPYRIGHT)

The overarching name for this project is Sky Sabre and the heart of this is the new Land Ceptor missile made by the European company, MBDA. The radar-guided Land Ceptor missiles are designed to provide point defence to important targets such as air bases, logistic sites, and headquarters.

Delivery of the first Sky Sabre to 16 Regiment RA began in late 2020 and during 2022 the first systems became operational in the Falklands. Later that year a small detachment was sent to Poland after the Russian invasion of Ukraine. A battery of the regiment also provides early warning of air attack with Saab G-AMB (Giraffe - Agile Multi Beam) surveillance radar and the wider Land Environment Air Picture Provision (LEAPP) network communication system.

The Starstreak HVM is the Royal Artillery's only close air defence weapon. It features a unique dart projectile rather than traditional high explosive warheads. Although these weapons have been deployed to conflicts in Iraq and Kosovo, as well as to protect the 2012 London Olympic Games, they have not been fired in anger by the British Army.

The British Army ordered the first Starstreak missiles from the then Shorts Missile Systems in

12 Regiment RA	
Formed	1947
Location	Thorney Island
Equipment	HVM Starstreak Missile/ Stormer vehicle

1986. The weapon was produced in three variants:

- Lightweight Missile Launcher (LML), with three missiles.
- Self-propelled (SP) on Stormer armoured vehicle, with eight missiles.
- Man portable, single missile.

The first missiles entered service in September 1997 and are currently only used by 12 Regiment Royal Artillery. British troops in Estonia are protected by a detachment of HVM. Britain has supplied Starstreak missiles to Ukraine and they are reported to have successfully shot down several Russian aircraft and helicopters.

The system and its launchers have been progressively improved. In 2000 new identification, friend or foe (IFF) equipment was incorporated. Seven years later Thales began work on the Starstreak II variant, which included increased range of 7km (4.3 miles), improved lethality, an improved targeting system, and much higher operating ceiling.

Reservists from 106 (Yeomanry) Regiment RA are earmarked to augment the regular units of 7 Air Defence Group.

16 Regiment RA	
Formed	1947
Location	Thorney Island
Equipment	Sky Sabre Missile System

106 (Yeomanry) Regiment RA	
Formed	1999
Location	London
Equipment	HVM Starstreak Missile

LEFT: Forward battlegroups are protected by the Starstreak High Velocity Missile air defence system. This is the man portable version. (MOD/CROWN COPYRIGHT)

BELOW: The Stormer armoured vehicle carried the Starstreak High Velocity Missile. It has seen action with the Ukrainian army. (MOD/CROWN COPYRIGHT)

32 Regiment RA

32 REGIMENT Royal Artillery was raised as 7 Medium Brigade RA at Clarence Barracks Portsmouth in 1927.

It is the British Army unit with the longest association with unmanned aerial vehicles (UAV) stretching back to the 1960s, when it first operated the jet powered Canadair CL-89 target locating drone.

In 1998 it became the first operator of the Phoenix UAV, which was the British Army's first modern UAV that incorporated a live video downlink. It took the Phoenix on operations to Kosovo in 1999, and then to Iraq between 2003 and 2006.

The Phoenix system was already obsolete by the time British troops deployed to Helmand province in Afghanistan in 2006, so the regiment was re-equipped first with the Desert Hawk mini-UAV, and then the Hermes 450 tactical UAV for the remainder of the Afghan campaign. The Hermes 450 was only a stopgap until the delayed Watchkeeper 450 fully entered service.

At the end of the Afghan campaign, the regiment focused on bringing the Watchkeeper fully into service until, in 2016, the British Army re-organised its UAV units. The regiment was switched to focusing on mini-UAVs with the Desert Hawk until 2020

when it was supposed to disband. However, it was given a reprieve when the decision was made to re-equip it with the US-made RQ-20 Puma and Wasp III mini UAVs. In 2023, it was announced that 250 more advanced systems would be purchased for the regiment to replace the Desert Hawks.

Small detachments of mini UAVs from 32 Regiment are routinely assigned to operate with British Army infantry and armoured battlegroups on training grounds around the UK and overseas. This unit reports to 1 Intelligence, Surveillance and Reconnaissance Brigade, alongside other signals intelligence and target acquisition units.

BELOW: The Puma mini UAV is used by detachments of 32 Regiment to provide close battlefield surveillance to units across the British Army. (MOD/CROWN COPYRIGHT)

32 Regiment RA	
First formed	1927
Location	Roberts Barracks, Larkhill
Aircraft	RQ-20 Puma and Wasp III AE (All Environment) mini unmanned air vehicle

47 Regiment RA

THE ROYAL Artillery's UAV force is concentrated on Salisbury Plan within the Larkhill Garrison complex. The Thales Watchkeeper WK450 is now operated by 47 Regiment Royal Artillery from its base at Larkhill. Local flying is conducted from the Ministry of Defence's Boscombe Down airfield and pilot training takes place at RAF Akrotiri on Cyprus, where the Mediterranean climate ensures flying can take place all year round. Test and evaluation flying is conducted from QinetiQ's airfield at Aberporth in west Wales.

In the summer of 2020, 47 Regiment was deployed on its first operational missions to monitor the English Channel for boats carrying migrants towards Dover from France. A forward operating location was set up at Lydd Airport for the patrols over the Channel, under the codename Operation Deveran.

The regiment was originally formed in 1947, as a coastal artillery training unit. It subsequently operated long-range rockets, field howitzers and air defence missiles, before converting to the Watchkeeper role in 2016, as part of a major reorganisation of the British Army's UAV units. At the same time, the Watchkeeper equipped regiment was moved under the day-to-day control of the Joint Helicopter Command to bring all army aviation assets under a single headquarters. As a result, in September 2019, the regiment changed from their black Royal Artillery headdress to that of the light blue Army Air Corps beret, although they retained their Gunner cap badge.

The Watchkeeper is undergoing a mid-life extension improvement project that will come online in 2026.

In October 2022, the regiment deployed its Watchkeepers to California to take part in trials under the banner of Project Convergence, alongside US and Australian forces to practice the integration of advanced sensors and new technologies to make the British Army more lethal on the battlefield, by cutting down on time and complications in what is called the 'sensor-decider-effector' chain.

BELOW: Royal Artillery personnel have regularly deployed to Lydd Airport in Kent to fly their Watchkeeper UAV in support of efforts by the Border Force to intercept migrant boat crossings. (MOD/CROWN COPYRIGHT)

47 Regiment RA	
First formed	1947
Locations	Horne Barracks, Larkhill, and Boscombe Down airfield
Aircraft	Watchkeeper Tactical UAV

Army Air Corps

1 Regiment AAC

1 REGIMENT AAC was formed at Hildesheim in Germany in January 1983, as the divisional anti-tank aviation regiment of 1 (UK) Armoured Division. It moved to Gutersloh in 1993, when it was still equipped with both Lynx and Gazelle helicopters and remained as the sole AAC regiment based in Germany. The classic Lynx AH7 and AH9 were progressively replaced by 34 upgraded AgustaWestland Wildcat AH1 from 2015 onwards. These new helicopters were concentrated in a single unit, 1 Regiment AAC, based at RNAS Yeovilton in Somerset in 2015.

Since then, all the land variants of the Wildcat are now operated as a single fleet, or pool, that is shared by 1 Regiment AAC and 847 Naval Air Squadron.

The AAC only has two operational Wildcat sub units, 661 and 659 Squadrons, and 652 Squadron is the training/conversion sub unit for the land variant.

The formation of the 1 Combat Aviation Brigade in April 2020 meant the Wildcats were placed in this organisation, alongside the AAC's Apache AH1 attack helicopters.

In 2018, 1 Regiment AAC began deploying detachments of Wildcats to the Baltic States to support NATO's enhanced forward presence battle groups. The size and frequency of these deployments have progressively increased, and they now regularly take their place as part of a joint aviation task force with AAC Apaches.

The regiment played an important role during the initial phase of the COVID-19 pandemic in 2020, flying teams of experts and high value cargo around the United Kingdom to support the National Health Service.

RIGHT: The AAC's Wildcat AH1 can be distinguished from Royal Navy Wildcat HMA2 by the lack of Sea Spray radar under the nose. It has been proposed to retrofit a radar to the Wildcat AH1s to increase their all weather surveillance capabilities.
(MOD/CROWN COPYRIGHT)

BELOW: RNAS Yeovilton is home to 1 Regiment AAC and the AAC's Wildcat AH1 fleet.
(MOD/CROWN COPYRIGHT)

1 Regiment AAC	
Home station	RNAS Yeovilton
Sub-units	661, 659 and 652 Squadrons
Current aircraft	Wildcat AH1

3 Regiment AAC

LEFT: 3 Regiment AAC is the lead unit for the entry to service of the upgraded AH-64E variant of the classic Apache attack helicopter. (MOD/CROWN COPYRIGHT)

3 REGIMENT AAC traces its roots back to 1969, when the British Army's 3rd Division required a dedicated aviation regiment to be formed. In 1976, following a reorganisation of the British Army of the Rhine (BOAR), the division's historic title was allocated to a newly established armoured formation based in the German town of Soest.

At the beginning of 1993, the regiment moved back to the UK and into the recently vacated RAF Station at Wattisham. In 1995, it was mobilised as the core of an Anglo-French rapid reaction force to support the United Nations Protection Force in the former Yugoslavia. Four years later, it became part of 16 Air Assault Brigade, as the UK's sole air manoeuvre formation.

When 3 Regiment AAC was mobilised to deploy to Kuwait ahead of the invasion of Iraq in early 2003, it still operated its legacy Westland Lynx AH7 and Westland Gazelle AH1s. This was the first time the AAC stood up as a battlegroup level unit for a major operation and many lessons were learned ahead of the actual fielding of the Westland Apache AH1 attack helicopter in 16 Brigade in 2004.

When 16 Brigade deployed to Helmand province in Afghanistan, it took Apaches from 9 Regiment AAC with it and they were immediately heavily engaged against Taliban insurgents. Over the next eight years, 3 Regiment AAC's squadron took turns to deploy for six months at a time to Camp Bastion in Afghanistan. In 2012 its most famous pilot, Prince Harry, served in Afghanistan.

In 2020, the regiment began to prepare to receive the new variant of the Apache, the Boeing AH-64E and the first of the new helicopters were flown to Wattisham in RAF Boeing C-17 Globemasters. Training is now at an advanced stage with the regiment's two squadrons fully converted. During 2023, the regiment will undergo its final collective training exercises, ahead of being declared fully operational in late 2023.

3 Regiment AAC	
Home station	Wattisham Flying Stations
Sub-units	662 and 663 Squadrons
Current aircraft	Boeing AH-64E Apache

BELOW: The AH-46E packs a powerful punch with Hellfire anti-armour missions, unguided rockets, and its nose mounted 30mm cannon. (MOD/CROWN COPYRIGHT)

4 Regiment AAC

ABOVE: 3 Regiment AAC is poised to begin converting from its legacy Apache AH1s to the new AH-64E variant this year.
(MOD/CROWN COPYRIGHT)

BELOW: In 2011, 3 Regiment AAC made history when they flew the first ever Apache combat missions from a warship, the helicopter carrier HMS *Ocean*, against land targets in Libya.
(MOD/CROWN COPYRIGHT)

4 REGIMENT AAC is one of two British Army aviation units in the attack helicopter role. It can trace its history back to 1969, when it stood up at Herford in Germany as the aviation regiment assigned to 4 Division.

The regiment was chosen to deploy to Saudi Arabia in late 1990 to be part of 1 (British) Armoured Division's artillery group for Operation Desert Storm. During the ground phase of the 1991 Gulf war its TOW-armed Lynx AH1 helicopters took part in first recorded combat use of the wire guided missile from a British helicopter.

4 Regiment AAC moved to its current home of Wattisham in 1994, and in September, 1999 became part of 16 Air Assault Brigade in anticipation of the introduction of the Westland Apache AH1 attack helicopter.

When 16 Brigade deployed to Helmand province in Afghanistan it took Apaches from 9 Regiment AAC with it, and they were in use immediately combatting Taliban forces. The need to keep a squadron of Apaches in Afghanistan to support subsequent rotations of British troops meant that over the next eight years, 3 Regiment AAC's squadrons took turns to deploy for six months at a time to Camp Bastion.

In the middle of the Afghan campaign, in May 2011, the regiment was alerted to provide a detachment of Apaches to embark on the helicopter carrier, HMS *Ocean*, to join the NATO-led air intervention in Libya. For four months, the Apache helicopters of 656 Squadron launched missions from the ship, as part of an Anglo-French attack operation. This was the first, and only time, UK Apache helicopters have flown from warships during combat operations. The mission was judged a success and the tactic is now routinely practiced in training, including from the new Queen Elizabeth class aircraft carriers.

4 Regiment AAC has taken on the bulk of Apache operation tasking while its sister unit converts to the new AH-64E variant, including deploying on short notice to eastern Europe in response to the Russian invasion of Ukraine in February 2022. It is scheduled to begin converting to the new helicopter in 2023 once 3 Regiment AAC is declared fully combat ready.

4 Regiment AAC	
Home station	Wattisham Flying Stations
Sub-units	656, 664 and 663 Squadrons
Current aircraft	Westland Apache AH1 (AH-64D)

5 Regiment AAC

5 REGIMENT AAC in Northern Ireland remains the sole British military unit operating the veteran Westland Gazelle AH1 utility observation helicopter, which first entered operational service with the AAC in 1974.

The regiment has only ever been based in Northern Ireland and was central to providing air support to the British Army and Royal Ulster Constabulary during the sectarian conflicts, known as 'The Troubles'. In 1979, the Northern Ireland Regiment of the AAC was formed to provide a formal command and administrative infrastructure to support flying operations in the province, centred at the RAF base at Aldergrove airport outside Belfast, and at the old RAF airfield at Ballykelly, near Londonderry.

In October 1993, the Northern Ireland Regiment was re-titled 5 Regiment AAC and progressively British air operations began to be concentrated at Aldergrove. After the 1998 Good Friday peace agreement the rotation of AAC squadrons ceased and, by 2007, the military ceased routine operations on the streets of the province.

Up to 2019, 5 Regiment AAC comprised two flying sub-units, 651 Squadron with the Britten-Norman

Islander AL1 and 665 Squadron with the Gazelle AH1. They provided specialist aviation support for the Police Service of Northern Ireland (PSNI) and counterterrorist police on the UK mainland. The Islanders were transferred to the RAF in 2019. The Gazelles are set to be retired in March 2024, ending the AAC career

of the Gazelle after more than 50 years in service.

5 Regiment AAC	
Home station	Aldergrove Flying Station
Sub-units	665 Squadron
Current aircraft	Westland Gazelle AH1

ABOVE: The veteran Gazelle AH1 provides manned aerial surveillance capability in support of the Police Service of Northern Ireland. (Airwolfhound)

LEFT: The Bell 212 was retired from AAC service in September 2022 when 667 Squadron in Brunei was disbanded. (MOD/CROWN COPYRIGHT)

Royal Engineers

Armoured Engineers

WHEN THE British Army wants to build something, blow something up, or clear a safe passage through a minefield or other obstacles, it calls the Royal Engineers. They are known as the Sappers because of their historic role digging trenches, or saps, in old style siege warfare.

In the 20th century the Royal Engineers developed a new form of combat engineering by fielding a family of specialist armoured vehicles that could lay bridges, clear lanes through minefields, dig trenches, bulldoze obstacles, and plant demolition charges on enemy field defences. They were dubbed 'Hobart's Funnies' after Major General Percy Hobart, who formed and commanded the famous 79th Armoured Division to spearhead the D-Day landings in Normandy.

The modern day successor of Hobart's Funnies are the two armoured engineer regiments of the Royal Engineers, assigned to 25 (Close Support) Engineer Group. They operate a range of specialist engineering vehicles.

25 (Close Support) Engineer Group	
Regiment/Unit	**Location**
HQ 25 (Close Support) Engineer Group	HQ Bulford
21 Regiment RE	Ripon
22 Regiment RE	Perham Down
26 Regiment RE	Perham Down
Royal Monmouthshire Royal Engineers (Militia)	Monmouth

The Trojan is an armoured engineer vehicle designed to open routes through complex battlefield obstacles and clear paths through minefields. It has a plough to clear routes though obstacles, can drop fascines to fill anti-tank ditches, an excavator arm to dig trenches, and a launcher to deploy the Python rocket-propelled mine clearing charge.

The Terrier armoured digger is the British Army's most advanced engineering vehicle, with a clamshell front bucket and side-mounted excavator arm which allows the vehicle to perform earth-moving and obstacle-removing tasks. A dismounted operator can also control the vehicle from up to 1,000 metres away.

Titan is an armoured engineer vehicle designed to enable troops and vehicles to cross gaps of up to 60m by laying a selection of close support bridges. Along with Trojan, it is based on the Challenger 2 tank chassis.

The armoured engineer squadrons of 22 and 26 Regiments RE have taken turns to deploy to Estonia as part of the NATO enhanced forward presence battlegroup.

More general engineering support to 3 (UK) Division is provided to 21 Engineer Regiment, which also includes the British Army's only amphibious engineering unit equipped with the M3 amphibious rig to cross wide water obstacles. Uniquely, 23 Amphibious Engineer Squadron, is based at Sennelager in Germany and is part of a joint bridging unit with the Germany army.

The M3 amphibious rig can be driven into a river and used as a ferry or, when a number are joined together from bank to bank, as a bridge, capable of taking vehicles as heavy as the Challenger 2 main battle tank. A single two-bay M3 can carry a 70-ton tracked vehicle, where two of its predecessor, the M2 would have been required for this task and required additional buoyancy bags. Eight M3 units and 24 soldiers can build a 100m bridge in 30 minutes.

25 (Close Support) Engineer Group reserve component is provided by the Royal Monmouthshire Royal Engineers (Militia), the most senior regiment of the Army Reserve, which can trace its history back to 1539.

LEFT: Titan is the Royal Engineer's armoured bridge-laying tank, and it is designed to allow the momentum of advance to be sustained by armoured battlegroups. (MOD/CROWN COPYRIGHT)

BELOW: The BAE Systems Trojan battlefield engineer vehicle is used in armoured battlegroups to clear obstacles in combat zones. (BAE SYSTEMS)

Force Support

THERE ARE now more than 7,000 Royal Engineers in the British Army and the majority of them serve in what are termed field squadrons within close support regiments, which are attached to light, light mechanised, air assault and amphibious brigades. They are trained and equipped to clear routes through minefields or other obstacles, build field fortifications, construct bridges over small rivers for troops and vehicles and undertake basic construction tasks to improve the living conditions on operations.

The largest Royal Engineer formation is 8 Engineer Brigade, which is part of 1 (UK) Division, and it has control of engineer units providing specialist force support. Its 12 Force Support Group has the task of providing theatre entry, route maintenance, and enabling airfield operations, with its two regular and two reserve close support regiments. It also has six specialist works teams, who are trained and equipped to build and maintain specialist infrastructure, such as aircraft hangers, runways, fuel storage facilities and water supply points.

12 Force Support Group	
Regiment/Unit	**Location**
HQ 12 Force Support Group	Wittering
36 (Queen's Gurkha Engineers) Regiment RE	Maidstone
39 Regiment RE	Kinloss
Army Reserve	
71 Regiment RE	Leuchars
75 Regiment RE	Warrington

LEFT: The Royal Engineers have formed a joint unit with the German army to operate the M3 bridging system to cross wide rivers. (BUNDESWEHR)

23 Parachute Regiment RE

THE AIRBORNE sappers of 23 Parachute Regiment RE are the dedicated engineering component of 16 Air Assault Brigade Combat Team. It comprises three regular and one reserve parachute trained squadron. The regiment is headquartered at Rock Barracks in Woodbridge, Suffolk. It is assigned to the UK's Global Response Force and is held at high readiness for rapid deployment. The unit's airborne sappers flew to Kabul in August 2021 to reinforce 16 Brigade defences during the British evacuation operation from the city's airport.

24 Commando Regiment RE

SPECIALIST SUPPORT for the amphibious operations conducted by 3 Commando Brigade is provided by the 24 Commando Regiment RE based at RMB Chivenor in Devon. The regiment's personnel are all trained as Army Commandos and are trained and equipped to participate in amphibious landings, including clearing beach obstacles, creating routes for vehicles off beaches and building field fortifications to protect bridgeheads.

32 Regiment RE

THE BRITISH Army's highly mobile 7 Light Mechanised Brigade Combat Team is supported by 32 Regiment RE from its base in Catterick. The regiment is to be part of NATO's Very High Readiness Joint Task Force in 2024.

Field plant, including JCBs and earth moving trucks, is used by the Royal Engineers for construction projects away from frontline areas. (TIM RIPLEY)

Specialist Engineers

AN IMPORTANT role of the Royal Engineers is the discovery and making safe of unexploded ordnance and improvised explosive devices. The role dates back to the Blitz of 1940 when bomb disposal teams of Royal Engineers were established around Britain to defuse unexploded German bombs.

The British Army and its sister services have since re-organised how this role is accomplished both within the UK and around the world. The Royal Logistic Corps Explosive Ordnance Disposal (EOD) has the lead in dealing with terrorist linked devices in the UK and left-over historic bombs from World War Two. They are assisted by Royal Navy divers in incidents below the tide line.

In overseas operations, the RLC EOD teams are assisted by Royal Engineer search teams who have the task of discovering suspect devices and then creating a safe route to allow the RLC operators to approach and make safe the device. Experts from the RE and RLC work closely together in this task, both to protect friendly forces and to preserve enemy devices for forensic examination. The two Royal Engineer EOD and search regiments are also trained and equipped to detect and make safe minefields and unexploded ordinance in war zones and have conducted this

ABOVE: The Royal Engineers maintain a stockpile of bridging equipment in co-operation with the defence company RBSL that can be used in wartime or for humanitarian tasks around the world.
(TIM RIPLEY)

important humanitarian task in the Falklands, Bosnia, Kosovo, Iraq, and Afghanistan.

In response to chemical weapon attacks in Syria and the infamous Salisbury Ricin poison attack in 2018 it was decided to enhance the British military's capabilities to deal with counter-chemical, biological, radiological, and nuclear (C-CBRN) events at home and abroad. 28 Regiment RE was set up in 2019 to lead efforts to contain and respond to poison gas and nuclear contamination incidents. It has the CBRN reconnaissance squadron of the Royal Tank Regiment under its command, with its armoured vehicles that can operate in contaminated areas.

Royal Engineer EOD and search regiments are grouped into 29 EOD & Search Group, headquartered at Didcot. It also controls RLC EOD units.

The Royal Engineers also have the job of providing the British Army's maps and this increasingly involves the use of digital map products, which are much in demand across the British armed forces. 42 Regiment RE is assigned to provide geographic support to the Defence Intelligence organisation's intelligence fusion centre at RAF Wyton.

The Royal School of Military Engineering at Chatham in Kent has been the home of the sappers for more than 150 years. It has specialist training organisations to cover combat engineering, construction engineering, EOD & search, operational tactics doctrine, as well as initial soldier and officer training.

LEFT: Royal Engineers officers receive training in the whole span of military engineering skills before specialising in specific areas.
(MOD/CROWN COPYRIGHT)

29 EOD & Search Group	
28 Regiment RE	Woodbridge & RAF Honington
33 Regiment RE	Carver Barracks, Wimbish
35 Regiment RE	Carver Barracks, Wimbish
11 (EOD & Search) Regiment RLC	Vauxhall Barracks, Didcot
101st (City of London) Regiment RE	London

Royal Logistic Corps

Support to Frontline

"AMATEURS TALK about tactics, professionals talk about logistics," was the phrase famously attributed to US Army General Omar Bradley during World War Two. This maxim has been taken to heart by the modern Royal Logistic Corps (RLC), which has the responsibility of keeping the supplies flowing to the British Army's frontline.

The modern RLC traces its roots back to the Royal Wagon Train, which was set up during the Napoleonic era. In 1993, the Royal Engineers Postal and Courier Service, Royal Corps of Transport, Royal Army Ordnance Corps, Royal Pioneer Corps and Army Catering Corps were merged to form the RLC.

It is the RLC's job to collect and then deliver everything the British Army needs to fight and operate in overseas theatres of operation. The bulk of RLC's 9,500 soldiers serve in logistics regiments that are assigned to support British Army armoured and infantry brigades. These regiments have squadrons of MAN trucks equipped with mechanical container/pallet loading systems, as well as fuel and water tankers. Their job is to collect ammunition, fuel, food and other bulk supplies from ports or major supply dumps and then deliver them to frontline battlegroups.

During static operations, logistics units are equipped to set up their own forward supply dumps or brigade administrative areas. When

supporting mobile operations, the logistics regiments have to load up their supply stocks on to their vehicles to ensure they are positioned close to the forward spearheads ready to resupply them between battles.

The 2021 Integrated Review re-organised the way the British Army conducts combat logistics. It

Support to 3 (UK) Division	
HQ 101 Operational Sustainment Brigade	Aldershot
27 Regiment RLC	Aldershot
10 Gurkha Regt RLC	Aldershot
151 (Greater London) Regiment RLC	Croydon
156 (North West) Regiment, RLC	Liverpool
157 (Welsh) Regiment RLC	Cardiff
12 Armoured Brigade Combat Team	
4 Regiment RLC	Abingdon
20 Armoured Brigade Combat Team	
1 Regiment RLC	Bicester

set up two sustainment brigades, which are assigned to support the two deployable formations, 1 (UK) and 3 (UK) Divisions, which were formed from the old 101 and 102 Logistic Brigades. Each brigade combat team was also assigned its own logistic regiment, although by necessity they have to co-ordinate their activities with the division sustainment brigade to ensure the smooth flow of supplies to the frontline.

As well as controlling RLC units, the sustainment brigade headquarters also command assigned Royal Army Medical Corps armoured ambulance units and Royal Electrical and Mechanical Engineer equipment repair workshops.

This concentration of all combat service and support units under a single headquarters allows logistic activity to be synchronised better with combat operations by frontline units.

The Army Reserve units have a central role in the modern RLC, and it is difficult to imagine that the British Army would be able to conduct a large-scale operation over a sustained period without the mobilisation of its reserve logistic units. Individual reservists also have an important role to augment regular units with personnel holding specialist trade qualifications, such as HGV drivers and bulk fuel handing.

LEFT: Since 2008 the Royal Logistic Corps has progressively replaced all its fleet of logistic vehicles with a new family of Support Vehicle, built by MAN Truck and Bus UK Ltd. The SV has seen service in Afghanistan and other theatres, often being fitted with enhanced armoured projection and defensive weapons.
(TIM RIPLEY)

BELOW: Cargo handling equipment, such as forklifts, is used by the Royal Logistic Corps to break down bulk items in smaller consignments to be distributed to fighting units in forward areas.
(MOD/CROWN COPYRIGHT)

Support to 1(UK) Division	
HQ 102 Operational Sustainment Brigade	Grantham
7 Regt RLC	Cottesmore
150 (Yorkshire) Regiment	Hull
159 Regiment RLC	Coventry
158 (Royal Anglian) Regiment RLC	Peterborough
4 Light Brigade Combat Team	
154 (Scottish) Logistic Regiment RLC	Dunfermline
7 Light Mechanised Brigade Combat Team	
6 Regiment RLC	Dishforth

Specialist Support

ABOVE: 17 Port and Maritime Regiment operates Mexeflote powered pontoons to unload ships and ferry vehicles across waterways. (MOD/COPYRIGHT)

THE BRITISH Army envisages deploying and operating far from its home base in Britain and the RLC has set up a dedicated theatre entry and sustainment brigade to conduct these specialist missions.

104 Theatre Sustainment Brigade has this task, and it has been assigned specialist RLC units to set up and sustain the British Army's supply chain overseas. There are two port regiments - one regular, 17 Regiment RLC, and one reserve, 165 Regiment - that are trained and equipped to load and unload cargo from ships at the Marchwood Military Port in Hampshire. It can also operate dock equipment in foreign ports to receive cargo, including shipping containers.

To control the movement of people and light cargo through air transport is the task of two movement control, postal and courier regiments. The hub for their operations is the Joint Air Mounting Centre at South Cerney in Gloucestershire, which is also the home garrison of 29 Postal Courier & Movement Regiment. It is supported by reservists of 162 Postal Courier & Movement Regiment.

152 (North Irish) Regiment RLC of the Army Reserve is the only dedicated Bulk Fuel Transport and Storage Regiment in the British Army. It operates a fleet of fuel tankers, which gives the regiment the capability to store and distribute bulk fuel anywhere in the world. Specialist

RIGHT: The loading and unloading of vehicles and heavy equipment at ports is a specialist capability that resides in 17 Port and Maritime Regiment and its reserve counterpart, 165 (Wessex) Port & Maritime Regiment. (MOD/CROWN COPYRIGHT)

104 Theatre Sustainment Brigade	
HQ 104 Theatre Sustainment Brigade	South Cerney
9 Regiment RLC	Hullavington
17 Port & Maritime Regiment RLC	Marchwood
29 Regiment RLC	South Cerney
152 (North Irish) Logistic Regiment RLC	Holywood
162 Logistic Regiment RLC	Nottingham
165 (Wessex) Port & Maritime Regiment RLC	Plymouth
167 Regiment RLC	Grantham

medical, fuel and supply support are also provided by the regular 9 Regiment RLC.

One of the most prominent roles of the RLC is to provide the British Army's chefs and they are attached to almost every one of its regiments and battalions. For major operations, units can draw chefs and catering specialists from 167 Regiment RLC.

As the successor to the old Royal Army Ordnance Corps (RAOC), the RLC is responsible for the safe storage and handling of all the British Army's munitions and explosives. This expertise led to them taking the lead in the disposal of road bombs in Northern Ireland during civil unrest known as 'The Troubles'. Its bomb disposal officers are known as Ammunition Technical Officers, or ATOs, To help it in its task, the RAOC spearheaded the development of robots, which were famously called 'wheelbarrows', to safely defuse bombs from a distance without putting human ATOs at risk. The RAOC also pioneered the protective suits that are now widely used by ATO's around the world. Modern RLC ATO's still use the 'Felix' radio call sign that originated in Northern Ireland in the 1970s.

The modern 11 EOD & Search Regiment RLC, headquartered at Didcot, is currently the British Army's lead specialist unit for dealing with terrorist bombs and legacy bombs left over from World War Two throughout Northern Ireland and mainland Britain. It also has teams dedicated to operating overseas in combat zones and for the conflicts in Iraq and Afghanistan the RLC fielded specialist armoured vehicles that contained an ATO's specialist equipment, including modern versions of the Wheelbarrow.

The regiment also inspects and licences ammunition storage, as well as enforcing explosives safety regulations across the British Army.

It has five squadrons based around Britain to ensure ATOs are able to rapidly responds to calls for assistance from police forces, emergency services and local authorities. These include:

- 321 EOD & Search Squadron – Aldergrove, Northern Ireland
- 421 EOD & Search Squadron – Didcot, Oxfordshire
- 521 EOD Squadron – Catterick Garrison, North Yorkshire
- 621 EOD Squadron – RAF Northolt, Middlesex
- 721 EOD Squadron –Ashchurch, Gloucestershire

The RLC provides 16 Air Assault Brigade Combat Team with

specialist logistic support to enable its role as Britain's Global Response Force. The Colchester-based 13 Air Assault Support Regiment has dedicated teams to support air manoeuvre operations, including loading cargo and pallets for delivery by helicopters and fixed wing transport aircraft. The regiment controls the British Army's only unit that prepares, loads, and dispatches cargo by parachute from RAF aircraft. The RAF Brize Norton-based 47 Air Despatch Squadron traces its history back to the first air dispatch units formed in World War Two to support airborne landings in D-Day and Arnhem.

The Logistic Support Squadron of the Commando Logistic Regiment at CMB Chivenor, includes a strong contingent of RLC personnel, whose role is to provide 3 Commando Brigade with second line logistic support that includes transport, stores, and bulk fuel during amphibious operations. It uses Demountable Rack Offload Pickup System (DROPS) vehicles to provide the lift needed to supply combat supplies, artillery ammunition and engineering equipment in bulk.

LEFT: The Troubles in Northern Ireland in the 1970s led the Royal Army Ordnance Corps to take on a lead role in countering terrorist bombs. (MOD/CROWN COPYRIGHT)

BELOW: The Gasket 3 bomb disposal robot is the Royal Logistic Corps' latest tool, which has evolved from the old Northern Ireland-era Wheelbarrow. (MOD/CROWN COPYRIGHT)

Royal Signals

Frontline Communications

WHEN THE first telegraphs began to revolutionise life during the Victorian era, the British Army sought to harness their power to rapidly pass information around the world.

The first signals unit was set up by the Royal Engineers in the 1870s to combine the use of signal flags, horse-mounted dispatch riders and telegraphs. During World War One the first radios were introduced, and motorcycles replaced horses in dispatch units. After the conflict, the modern Royal Corps of Signals was formed.

Today, the Royal Signals have an array of tasks that goes beyond just being responsible for radio communications. Its main signals regiments and signals squadrons effectively provide the core element of each army divisional and brigade headquarters. Signallers drive the headquarters vehicles, set up the command posts and operate all their radio, computer, and data networks.

Communications within infantry or armoured battlegroups, as well as artillery, logistics and engineer regiments, are run by those units themselves, not specialist personnel from the Royal Signals. However, radio operators across the British Army are still referred to as signallers even if they are not members of the Royal Signals.

The core of 3 (UK) Division headquarters is its signals regiment, 3 Regiment, and each of its two armoured brigades are supported by their own signals regiment.

1 (UK) Division has fewer resources, with its 2 Signals Regiment supporting its divisional headquarters and its two component manoeuvre brigades. Communications for 16 Air Assault Brigade Combat Team is provided

ABOVE: Air-to-ground communication nets are run by the Royal Signals, using a mix of voice radios, satellite, and data links. (MOD/CROWN COPYRIGHT)

by 216 Signals Squadron, which is trained to be inserted by parachute during rapid reaction missions.

The Royal Signals are also responsible for gathering intelligence from enemy radio communications and a dedicated tactical signals intelligence (SIGINT) unit, 14 Signals Regiment, has specialist equipment to monitor enemy radio traffic and pinpoint the location of enemy radio transmitters. The Royal Signals also contribute to strategic SIGINT activity by the Britain's national eavesdropping agency, GCHQ, including providing personnel for the Joint Service Signal Unit at the Ayios Nikolaos intelligence base on Cyprus.

Increasingly, the Royal Signals are taking on frontline roles to protect the British Army's computer systems from cyber attack. The Royal Signals are now part of the National Cyber Force which also has an offensive role against the computer systems of terrorist groups or hostile states.

The 2021 Integrated Review expanded the role of Royal Signals in these increasingly important domains by setting up the Electronic Warfare & Cyber Effects Group to better integrate their activities.

During the conflicts in Iraq and Afghanistan, Royal Signals teams also monitored and jammed insurgent radio-controlled roadside bombs. Since 2021, a dedicated Royal Signals unit, 660 Signals Troop, has been established within 29 EOD & Search Group to expand this role.

BELOW: The Royal Signals were on parade in strength for King Charles III's coronation ceremony in London on May 6, 2023. (MOD/CROWN COPYRIGHT)

Information and Communication Services for 3 (UK) Division	
Unit	Location
Regular Army	
HQ 7 Signals Group	Stafford
1 Signal Regiment	Stafford
3 Signal Regiment	Bulford
15 Signal Regiment	Blandford Camp
Army Reserve	
71 (City of London) Yeomanry Signal Regiment	London
Information and Communication Services for 1 (UK) Division	
Regular Army	
2 Signal Regiment	Imphal Barracks
Army Reserve	
37 Signal Regiment	Redditch
Electronic Warfare & Cyber Effects Group	
13 Signal Regiment	Blandford Camp
14 (Electronic Warfare) Signal Regiment	Cawdor Barracks
21 Signal Regiment	Colerne

Strategic Communications

TO ALLOW the British Army to project power around the world, it needs capable and secure communications. The Royal Signals have the mission of providing the strategic communications for the British Army and elements of the other armed services. In this role, the Royal Signals relies heavily on satellite communications, but it does not own or operate satellites. They are provided by the Ministry of Defence through its Skynet constellations, or via leased services from commercial companies.

The British Army satellite communications come in the shape of high-capacity networks that use large satellite dishes that have to be mounted on trailers towed by vehicles. As a result, they are largely restricted to use by main headquarters units. Small man portable satellite radios are also in widespread use with tactical units.

The 2021 Integrated Review reorganised the British Army's strategic communications units, bringing them under the control of 1 Signals Brigade. Its main customer

is the Headquarters Allied Rapid Reaction Corps, which is the British Army's deployable three-star land component headquarters. The Brigade also provides units and personnel at high readiness to deploy to support the UK Permanent Joint Headquarters (PJHQ), the Joint Helicopter Force and other government departments,

such as the disaster relief teams of the Foreign, Commonwealth and Development Office.

22 Signal Regiment provides the information communications systems to enable commander ARRC to exercise command over his Corps' British and allied component units. To sustain and support the ARRC Headquarters,

RIGHT: The Falcon network communication system mounted in MAN vehicles. It is to be replaced by a new Trinity system later this decade. (MOD/CROWN COPYRIGHT)

BELOW: The Allied Rapid Reaction Corps (ARRC) headquarters is supported by 1 Signals Brigade and its satellite communication systems. (MOD/CROWN COPYRIGHT)

communication to army headquarters and defence locations around the United Kingdom, for resilience and national security operations. Reserve units of 32 and 39 Signals Regiments support this role.

The global operations of the UK Special Forces Group are supported by the specialist communicators of 18 Signal Regiment, which has access to a unique communication systems and technology.

All Royal Signals personnel receive their initial trade training at the Royal School of Signals at Blandford but later can receive more specialist skills at specialist training establishments across the British Army, other armed forces, and specialist agencies.

LEFT: The Royal Signals have the satellite communications equipment to connect British Army units wherever they are in the world. (MOD/CROWN COPYRIGHT)

1 Signals Brigade also controls the Gurkha ARRC Support Battalion and the ARRC Military Police Battalion of the Royal Military Police. They provide life support, security, and force protection for the ARRC Headquarters when it deploys into the field.

30 Signal Regiment is responsible for enabling PJHQ's deployable Joint Force Headquarters and supporting other high readiness formations, such as the very high readiness field hospital, the air manoeuvre battlegroup of 16 Air Assault Brigade Combat Team and Joint Helicopter Command. 299 Signal Squadron (Special Communications) provides specialist communications support to the Foreign, Commonwealth and Development Office.

10 Signals Regiment has a unique role, providing national

Support for HQ Allied Rapid Reaction Corps	
Unit	**Location**
Regular Army	
HQ 1st Signals Brigade	Innsworth
10 Signal Regiment	Corsham
16 Signal Regiment	Stafford
22 Signal Regiment	Stafford
30 Queen's Gurkha Signal Regiment	Bramcote
Army Reserve	
32 Signal Regiment	Glasgow
39 Signal Regiment	Bristol
Royal School of Signals	
Unit	**Location**
11 Signal Regiment	Blandford Camp
Special Forces Support	
Unit	**Location**
18 (United Kingdom Special Forces) Signal Regiment	Credenhill

BELOW: In January 2023, 1 Signals Brigade deployed to RAF St Mawgan to practice deploying and establishing communications for the Allied Rapid Reaction Corps (ARRC). (MOD/CROWN COPYRIGHT)

Royal Army Medical Corps

The Army's Combat Lifeline

Looking after the health of the British Army is the job of the 4,000 regular personnel of the Army Medical Services (AMS). Its components include the Royal Army Medical Corps, the Royal Army Dental Corps, and the Queen Alexandra's Royal Army Nursing Corps. At home garrisons the AMS provides routine medical services for soldiers and their families but stands ready to rapidly expand its operations in time of conflict, often with the support of reservists, to set up field hospitals in war zones.

The AMS has a portfolio of units and capabilities to allow it to support a range of operational scenarios, from a small-scale operation involving a company of 100 or so troops to divisional level operations by thousands of personnel.

British medical doctrine says the principal task of the AMS is to maintain the fighting strength of a deployed force by preventing disease and other non-battle injuries as well as tending to the sick and wounded. Rapid and efficient evacuation and treatment is seen by the British Army as the key to maintaining the morale and fighting spirit of its soldiers.

Medical support is provided according to a range of requirements:
- Role 1 provides medical sections and unit aid posts. This is provided by battalion and regimental sized unit's own medical personnel.

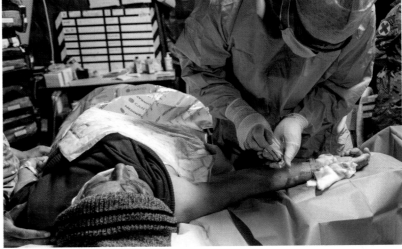

- Role 2 light manoeuvre facilities conduct triage and advanced resuscitation procedures, up to damage control surgery. This is provided by close support medical regiments of the RMAC, which used to be called armoured or field ambulance units. This can be enhanced with specialist surgical and nursing teams in forward locations for limited periods.
- Role 3 medical treatment facilities provide secondary care on operations to high clinical standards. These are provided by RAMC regular and reserve field hospitals units.

Royal Army Medical Corps (RAMC), Major Units 2023

Unit type	Specialty	Home base
Regular Army		
1 Armoured Medical Regiment RAMC	Armoured Ambulance/20 Armoured BCT	Tidworth
3 Medical Regiment RAMC	to disband	Preston
4 Armoured Regiment RAMC (to 2 Medical Regiment (RAMC)	Armoured Ambulance/12 Armoured BCT	Aldershot
5 Armoured Regiment RAMC (to 3 Medical Regiment (RAMC)	Close Support/7 Light Mech BCT	Catterick
16 Medical Regiment RAMC	Close Support/16 Air Assault BCT	Colchester
22 Field Hospital (to 22 Multi-role Medical Regiment RAMC)	Field Hospital	Aldershot
34 Field Hospital (to 21 Multi-role Medical Regiment RAMC)	Field Hospital	York
Army Reserve		
201 (Northern) Field Hospital (to 214 (North East) Multi-role Medical Regiment RAMC)	Field Hospital	Newcastle
202 (Midlands) Field Hospital (to 202 (Midlands) Multi-role Medical Regiment RAMC)	Field Hospital	Birmingham
203 (Welsh) Field Hospital (to 203 (Welsh) Multi-role Medical Regiment RAMC)	Field Hospital	Cardiff
204 (North Irish) Field Hospital (to 214 (North Irish) Multi-role Medical Regiment RAMC)	Field Hospital	Belfast
205 (Scottish) Field Hospital (to 215 (Scottish) Multi-role Medical Regiment RAMC)	Field Hospital	Glasgow
206 (North West) Multi-role Medical Regiment RAMC	Field Hospital	Manchester/Liverpool
212 (Yorkshire) Field Hospital (to 214 (North East) Multi-role Medical Regiment RAMC)	Field Hospital	Sheffield
243 (The Wessex) Field Hospital (to 243 (Wessex) Multi-role Medical Regiment RAMC)	Field Hospital	Keynsham
254 (East of England) Multi-role Medical Regiment RAMC	Field Hospital	Cambridge
256 (City of London) Field Hospital (to 256 (London) Multi-role Medical Regiment RAMC)	Field Hospital	Walworth
306 Hospital Support Regiment RAMC	Field Hospital Operations	Strensall
335 Medical Evacuation Regiment RAMC	Ambulance Operations	Strensall

- Role 4 medical facilities, usually in the strategic base, receive patients from operations. Such facilities also provide access to definitive and specialist care and rehabilitation. This is currently provided by the National Health Service and the Defence and National Rehabilitation Centre (DNRC) at Stanford Hall.

AMS personnel and units provide all the above capabilities and also contribute to land and airborne evacuation chains to move wounded soldiers from the frontline back to more suitable treatment facilities. This is either by armoured ambulances or in helicopters, with a medical emergency response team (MERT)

LEFT: Foreign Commonwealth and Development Office minister, Andrew Mitchell visits 13 Medical Regiment's field hospital in Turkey, which spearheaded the UK's response to the devastating earthquake in the country in February 2023.
(MOD/CROWN COPYRIGHT)

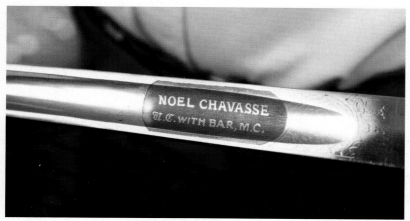

onboard to stabilise casualties en route to field hospitals.

The campaign in Afghanistan saw the AMS, supported by Royal Air Force and Royal Navy colleagues, establish a Role 3 hospital at Camp Bastion and relied largely on a helicopter-borne evacuation chain.

In the 2021 Integrated Review, a programme to reorganise and streamline the main AMS units was set in train. This envisages the old field hospital units being renamed multi-role medical regiments. The bulk of the amalgamations are set to take place in 2024.

LEFT: Two of the three British servicemen to win the Victoria Cross twice have been army doctors. In honour of RAMC Captain Noel Chavasse, who was the only double Victoria Cross winner in World War One, RAMC Colonel Graham Johnson carried his sword in King Charles III's coronation parade on May 6, 2023.
(MOD/CROWN COPYRIGHT)

Specialist Units

Expert Support

The British Army relies on the skills and expertise of multiple specialist units and personnel to keep it fighting and operating around the world, in extreme climates and environments.

Royal Electrical and Mechanical Engineers

KEEPING THE British Army's weapons, vehicles, and helicopters in working order is the responsibility of the Royal Electrical and Mechanical Engineers, or REME.

Royal Electrical and Mechanical Engineers (REME)		
Unit	**Brigade**	**Location**
1 Close Support Battalion	Light Mech BCT	Catterick
2 Close Support Battalion	102 OSB	Leuchars
3 Close Support Battalion	20 Armoured BCT	Tidworth
4 Close Support Battalion	12 Armoured BCT	Tidworth
5 Field Support Battalion	101 OSB	Lyneham
6 Close Support Battalion	1 Deep Recce Strike BCT	Tidworth
7 Battalion REME	1 Aviation BCT	Wattisham

ABOVE: Vehicle mechanics from the Royal Electrical and Mechanical Engineers keep the British Army rolling.
(MOD/CROWN COPYRIGHT)

Adjutant General's Corps

THE ADMINISTRATION of soldiers' pay and other documentation is done by the Adjutant General's Corps, which also contains the famous Red Caps of the Royal Military Police.

The British Army's prison, the Military Corrective Training Centre at Colchester, is run by the personnel of the Military Prison Staff Corps (MPSC).

Royal Military Police	
Unit	**Location**
1 Regiment RMP	Catterick
3 Regiment RMP	Bulford
ARRC Military Police Battalion	Winchester

RIGHT: Royal Military Police officers are often the public face of the British Army helping to providing security at major events but during King Charles III coronation ceremony on May 6, 2023, a contingent of Red Caps found themselves on parade.
(MOD/CROWN COPYRIGHT)

Intelligence Corps

MONITORING ENEMY troop movements and understanding the capabilities of hostile weapon systems is done by the Intelligence Corps, which is also responsible for the interrogation of enemy prisoners of war.

Intelligence Corps		
Unit	**Division**	**Location**
Regular Army		
1 Military Intelligence Battalion	1 (UK) Division	Catterick
2 Military Intelligence Battalion	ISR Group	Upavon
4 Military Intelligence Battalion	3 (UK) Division	Bulford
Army Reserve		
3 Military Intelligence Battalion	ISR Group	London
5 Military Intelligence Battalion	1 (UK) Division	Edinburgh
6 Military Intelligence Battalion	77 Brigade	Manchester
7 Military Intelligence Battalion	3 (UK) Division	Bristol

LEFT: Search and guard dogs are used by the British Army in most operational theatres. They are provided by Royal Army Veterinary Corps, with more than 300 dogs usually in service in recent years. (MOD/CROWN COPYRIGHT)

Royal Army Veterinary Corps (RAVC)	
1 Working Dog Regiment	North Luffenham

Musicians, Vets, and Vicars

MILITARY BANDS are a major part of British Army life, providing stirring music for royal events, national celebrations, and regimental activities. There are now 14 bands in the regular component of the Royal Corps of Army Music, containing just over 750 musicians.

The health of the army's guard and search dogs, as well the horses of ceremonial units, is the responsibility of the 330 personnel of the Royal Army Veterinary Corps, while the Royal Army Physical Training Corps makes sure the soldiers are fit to fight. The spiritual wellbeing of soldiers is looked after by the Royal Army Chaplains Department, which provides 120 padres from many religious denominations to work in army units.

Royal Corps of Army Music	
Band	**Location**
Band of the Household Cavalry	Windsor
Band of the Grenadier Guards	London
Band of the Coldstream Guards	London
Band of the Scots Guards	London
Band of the Irish Guards	London
Band of the Welsh Guards	London
Band of the Royal Regiment of Scotland	Edinburgh
Band and Bugles of The Rifles	Winchester
Countess of Wessex's String Orchestra	Woolwich Station, London
British Army Band	Catterick
British Army Band	Tidworth
British Army Band	Sandhurst
British Army Band	Colchester
Band of the Prince of Wales	Brecon

BELOW: British military music is integral to both the army's history and modern ethos. Here the Band of the Welsh Guards performs at King Charles III coronation ceremony on May 6, 2023. (MOD/CROWN COPYRIGHT)

Looking Ahead

A British Army for the 21st Century?

There are many ways to look at the British Army in 2023. At 75,000 trained soldiers, it is undoubtedly the case that the British Army is the smallest its has been in 200 years. Only 25 years ago, the British Army boasted 110,000 regular soldiers. So not surprisingly, politicians, think tank commentators and media pundits regularly lambast the continually shrinking size of the British Army.

Does this mean the British Army is less capable and can do less that it could in 1998? On the surface, that seems self evident. If it has less soldiers, the British Army can do less.

RIGHT: Close quarter combat skills – including throwing hand grenades – are still needed by the British Army's infantry soldiers.
(MOD/CROWN COPYRIGHT)

When compared to the British Army in 1998, after the New Labour Strategic Defence Review the British Army had two deployment divisions, each with three full brigades with armoured or mechanised battlegroups. Today the British Army still has two deployable divisions, but they only have two brigades each and the armoured division only has two brigades equipped with tanks and tracked armoured vehicles.

Enablers

But modern warfare is not just about tanks and infantry soldiers. Battles are now won and lost by what are called enablers – drones, bomb disposal engineers, attack helicopters, and electronic warfare to jam the enemy's communications. The British Army in 2023 has more and far better enablers that its predecessor did in 1998. Then the British Army had no functioning drones to provide an 'eye in the sky', it had not yet taken delivery of its first Westland Apache AH1 attack helicopter and had no effective radars to track enemy artillery and mortar fire. Its light armoured vehicles were soon found to be highly vulnerable to insurgent roadside bombs in Iraq.

This situation has been turned around and the British Army now has some of the world's best battlefield enablers. It is refreshing its fleet of attack helicopters, has highly effect mine resistance ambush protected (MRAP) vehicles, Giraffe and MAMBA battlefield radars, Watchkeeper, Puma and Wasp drones, new bomb disposal radars and has started to take delivery of the Sky Sabre air defence system.

Many of these capabilities were purchased after hard lessons were learnt in Iraq and Afghanistan about the importance of enablers »

BELOW: An improved version of the Challenger main tank is being developed RBSL in Telford. (TIM RIPLEY)

in securing battlefield success and, crucially, limiting casualties.

The British Army is now in the process of refreshing its main combat vehicles, by bringing the Boxer armoured personnel carrier and Challenger 3 main battle tank into service over the remainder of the decade.

Fighting Fit?

So, is the new look British Army fit to fight 21st century opponents? Fighting power is not just about having the right kit and weapons. It needs effective organisation , battle winning tactics, effective logistics, good leaders, and a will to win.

The British Army contains a strong cadre of leaders – officers and senior

NCOs – who have amassed decades of operational experience in Iraq, Afghanistan and elsewhere. It has fought several tough and complex campaigns, requiring its leaders to innovate to overcome determined and well-equipped enemies. So, when it comes to what is called the 'moral component' - leadership and morale – the British Army is strong.

It is more than 20 years since the British Army fought an armoured battle on the streets of Basra and even then, the Iraqis could only field 1960s vintage T-55 tanks against the Challenger 2 tanks of 7 Armoured Brigade. Not a single British tank was penetrated by enemy fire during the Battle of Basra. Even in the 1991 Gulf war when the British Army

faced better equipped and motivated Iraqi forces, coalition air power did the hard yards and reduced the combat effectiveness of Saddam Hussein's army by 50% even before a single coalition tank crossed the start line.

So, the British Army undoubtedly is behind the curve when it comes to high intensity armoured warfare. There is a good number of officers and senior NCOs who fought in Basra in 2003 still in the ranks, but hardly anyone from the 1991 Gulf War. Not surprisingly, the British Army has launched a major effort to learn as much as possible about the Ukrainian and Russian armies that have been fighting and operating over the past 18 months.

There are obvious lessons to learn about how tanks and artillery can operate successfully in an environment where small aerial drones can almost instantly track them. The role of electronic warfare in defeating drone surveillance is also a key area for investigation.

How modern air defences neutralise air power is another important area where things have changed dramatically over the past 30 years.

New Lessons
The Ukraine war is also having a huge impact on how artillery is

employed. Over the past 30 years the British Army was predominately used in a counter-insurgency role, so precision weapons had priority to minimise civilian casualties as part of a drive to win 'hearts and minds' of local populations. In Ukraine, old fashioned massed artillery barraged »

ABOVE: British soldiers are increasingly deploying to the Pacific region for joint training with old and new allies. In 2022 the Parachute Regiment sent troops to Japan to train with the Japan Self-Defense Force. (MOD/CROWN COPYRIGHT)

to neutralise whole sections of frontline for prolonged periods have made a comeback. Tens of thousands of shells a day were fired during some battles in Ukraine.

To operate in this environment, the British Army will have look again at the number of artillery pieces and, perhaps more importantly, its stockpile of shells and the number of trucks in the Royal Logistic Corps to move them to frontline gun lines.

To date, the British Army has not declared it has the answer to many of these questions and is in the midst of a major period of experimentation to assess rival concepts and new equipment in a number of tactical scenarios.

This is all to be expected, but as the sudden start of the Ukraine war last year showed, the world is very unstable, and the British Army might not have much time to get its act together before it is called into action. Sometimes nations and armies don't get to choose which army they fight but have to respond rapidly to unexpected events. It the third decade of the 21st century, the British Army does not have the luxury of studying future warfare trends in a leisurely and deliberate way. A more rapid and determined effort is needed to quickly make choices and find solutions.

In June 2022, General Sir Patrick Sanders, the head of the British Army told the Royal United Services Institute think tank that Britain faced what he called a '1937 moment'. This was an analogy with the countdown to start of World War Two and the need to accelerate rearmament.

It is a year since the General made his speech, and progress appears to be slow in speeding up efforts to rebuilding and reorganising the British Army. In Afghanistan, a Taliban commander once reportedly told a NATO general: "You have the watches, but we have the time." Time may not be luxury that the British Army has any more.